Autism
From theoretical understanding to educational intervention

Autism
From theoretical understanding to
educational intervention

Theo Peeters
Centre for Training Professionals
in Autism, Antwerp

Whurr Publishers Ltd
London

©1997 Whurr Publishers Ltd

First published in English 1997 by
Whurr Publishers Ltd
19B Compton Terrace, London N1 2UN, England

British Library Cataloguing-in-Publication Data
A catalogue record for this book is available from the
British Library.

ISBN 1 86156 003 6

Eerste druk april 1994
Tweede druk april 1995

Copyright © Theo Peeters/Uitgeverij Hadewijch, 1994
Uitgeverij Hadewijch Antwerpen-Baarn
Omslag Herman Houbrechts

ISBN 90 5240 230 2
D 1995 4237 13
NUGI-code 711/725

Verspreiding voor België: Westland nv, Schoten
Verspreiding voor Nederland: Combo-distributiecentrum
van Bosch en Keuning nv, Baarn

Printed and bound in the UK by Athenaeum Press Ltd,
Gateshead, Tyne and Wear

Contents

Dedication

For M., S., M. and the Z.v.A.

Being autistic does not mean being inhuman. But it does mean being alien. It means that what is normal for other people is not normal for me, and what is normal for me is not normal for other people. In some ways I am terribly ill-equipped to survive in this world, like an extra-terrestrial stranded without an orientation manual.

But my personhood is intact. My selfhood is undamaged. I find value and meaning in life, and I have no wish to be cured of being myself . . . Grant me the dignity of meeting me on my own terms . . . Recognise that we are equally alien to each other, that my ways of being are not merely damaged versions of yours. Question your assumptions. Define your terms. Work with me to build bridges between us. Jim Sinclair, 1992.

Preface

I wrote this book because it had to be written. The links between theoretical knowledge and educational intervention for people with autism is often insufficiently understood.

The most important impulse for writing this book came from the European Conference of Parents' Associations in Hamburg (Autism: Today and Tomorrow May 6–8, 1988). It was an important conference because in a broad European context it clearly bade farewell to the psychogenetic interpretations of autism and opted instead for treatment using educational strategies. But within this 'organic educational' orientation there were so many different slants that many professionals and, of course, parents felt somewhat lost: where was the wood and where were the trees?

There often seemed to be a huge gap between theory and practice. Theorists give interesting speeches, but what was their relevance to, for example, teachers? Between the various meetings, one heard teachers and other professionals airing their doubts: they had already been forced to try many different methods and therapies and now they were asking themselves why. Parents were only too used to such a general lack of direction. No effort was too much for them, but there is nothing more exhausting than battling in a void where you do not really understand the whys and wherefores. I believe that professionals and parents need a sort of 'working philosophy' of autism: a paradigm that builds a bridge between theory and practice.

In the worst case we might land in a kind of autism supermarket where all the different approaches to autism are displayed together, with room for all (a little holding therapy, a little option method and a little delacato; in other words, a cocktail). This is not a plea against openness – quite the contrary – but no-one with autism can survive in a maze where one approach is accepted as well as its opposite.

The theories defended in this book have an established scientific base, and this also has implications when they are put into practice.

At the moment autism is the most well-documented and most well-understood syndrome in child psychiatry. More articles and books have been written on autism in the West than there are children with autism. There is, then, some insight into the subject (you will find it in this book): the days when it was possible to hide behind 'the riddle of autism' are over.

In this book I attempt to explain the link between a theoretical understanding of autism and its consequences for education. I attempt to pass on a working philosophy for professional carers from which they can develop an educational methodology. Five important theoretical concepts are explained, one in each chapter, and each is followed by a general discussion of practical application.

This book was intended for a broad public; it is meant to be informative rather than academic. For this reason I have intentionally avoided inserting too many bibliographic references in the text, which might slow the reader down. However, I have, of course, drawn on many sources for my information. The interested reader will find a select bibliography at the end of the book for further reading.

I am happy to be able to illustrate more fully the points made in this book with so many striking examples. In earlier publications I was criticized for drawing on too many examples from 'low-functioning' persons with autism. This time the reaction is likely to be the opposite. In recent years numerous high-functioning individuals with autism have had their say in all sorts of publications. They are witnesses to the fact that we professionals are on the right track with our insights; sometimes they also helped to sharpen the focus of our insights or to adapt them.

I must also give special thanks to Hilde De Clercq and Cis Schiltmans for allowing me to use so many of their moving anecdotes and to Francesca Happé, Rita Jordan and Stuart Powell for the useful comments. Thank you also to my daughter, Maya, who made some of the drawings.

The supplement on 'Ian' can be taken by the reader as a reward for studying this book. It seems to me to be written so completely from the heart, and to contain so much wisdom and tenderness, that it seemed unethical to keep it to myself.

This book also hopes to contribute by breathing new life into work with autism. At the moment we find ourselves in a sort of deadlock between professionals who believe in a specific autism approach and authorities who are not sufficiently aware that the problems of autism cannot be solved by training alone. Autism is not only an educational problem, it is also a political one. Understanding educational strategies to help people with autism is all well and good, but to put these educational strategies into practice demands suitable means.

Chapter 1
Autism as a pervasive developmental disorder

1. Theoretical understanding

1.1. What is autism? How many people are affected?

How do you know if someone has autism?

For this you must call on criteria defined by the medical profession. The criteria most often used are those of the World Health Organization, recorded in the ICD-10 (International Classification of Disease, 10th edn. (WHO, 1987) and the DSM-IV (Diagnostic Statistical Manual, 4th edn. developed by the American Psychiatric Association) (APA, 1994).

The definition of the autistic disorder in the DSM IV goes as follows:

A. A total of at least six items from Groups 1, 2 and 3 including at least two items from Group 1, at least one item from Group 2 at least one item from Group 3.

1. Qualitative impairment in social interaction as manifested by at least two of the following:
   a. Marked impairment in the use of multiple nonverbal behaviours such as eye-to-eye gaze, facial expression, body postures, and gestures to regulate social interaction
   b. Failure to develop peer relationships appropriate to developmental level
   c. Markedly impaired experience of pleasure in other people's happiness
   d. Lack of social–emotional reciprocity

2. Qualitative impairments in communication as manifested by at least one of the following:
   a. A delay in, or total lack of development of spoken language (not accompanied by an attempt to compensate through the use of gesture or mime as alternative modes of communication)

  b. Marked impairment in the ability to initiate or sustain a conversation with others despite adequate speech
  c. Stereotyped and repetitive use of language or idiosyncratic language
  d. Lack of varied spontaneous make-believe play or social imitative play appropriate to developmental level

3. Restricted, repetitive, and stereotyped patterns of behaviour interest as manifested by at least one of the following:
  a. Encompassing preoccupation with one or more stereotyped and restricted patterns of interest abnormal either in intensity or focus
  b. An apparently compulsive adherence to specific nonfunctional routines or rituals
  c. Stereotyped and repetitive motor mannerisms (e.g. hand or finger flapping or twisting or complex whole body movements)
  d. Persistent preoccupation with parts of objects

B. Abnormal or impaired development prior to age 3 as manifested by delays or abnormal functioning in at least one of the following areas: (1) social interaction, language used in social development,(2) language as used in social communication, or (3) symbolic or imaginative play.

C. Not better accounted for by Rett Disorder, Childhood Integrative Disorder, or Asperger Syndrome.

It was previously thought that five out of 10 000 people were autistic, but recent epidemiological research, using the DSM III-R criteria, has led to that figure being doubled to 10 in 10 000.

If one uses an educational definition of autism (including youngsters with autism and related disorders) instead of a medical (until now it has been mainly the medical profession who have provided the criteria used) there are at least 20 in every 10 000 people affected.

1.2 The family of mental retardation and learning disorders

In the DSM IV (just as in the ICD-10) autism is placed under the category 'pervasive developmental disorders', between 'mental retardation' and 'specific developmental disorders'.

Under 'mental retardation', it may be said that development is slowed down. Someone who is mentally retarded develops along the same lines as you and me, but more slowly. His mental age is always lower than his chronological age.

Under 'specific developmental disorders' we are faced with slow or faulty development in one particular skill area. Someone with dyslexia, for example, has one exceptional learning difficulty. Although he is of normal intelligence, he has unusual difficulty in learning to read.

Where there are several areas of 'qualitative impairments' we refer to a 'pervasive development disorder'. A pervasive development disorder such as autism is, then, classified as lying between mental retardation and learning disorders. The most important characteristic of the pervasive development disorder group is that 'the dominant disorders consist of difficulties in acquiring cognitive, language, motor and social skills'. By the term 'qualitative impairments' we understand that the impairments may be due to more than just slow development (as is the case with mental retardation) or a secondary handicap (sensory or motor). The following anecdote on the preparation of a Christmas party illustrates these qualitative limitations, this 'other' development.

> The festive season is coming around again with all its surprises. I'm really not looking forward to it because Thomas's daily routine is disturbed. But I have found one way of helping him: for most of us a surprise is usually nice, but for him things are only nice if they're predictable. So I show him the advertising brochures with the toy that Santa Claus will bring, what he can do with the toy, how he can use it. We cut out all the pictures and stick them on pieces of paper. I make him a calendar with white pages so he can tear them off himself, one every day. He can see exactly how long it will be. And we stick the picture with the surprise on a sheet of red paper. We then go to the shop to look at the real present because it doesn't look exactly the same as the one in the advertisement. And if we can, we borrow it from the toy library so I'm sure that it isn't too difficult for him and that he can work it.
>
> The night before Christmas I tell him where he can find the 'surprise', and in what kind of paper it will be wrapped. His brothers and sisters think that half the fun is lost if they know about things beforehand. But when the big day comes and the red sheet turns up on his calendar, it is a real party for ALL the children. Even for Thomas because now he doesn't fling the paper on the ground, doesn't scream or cry. He has found what he expected, it was predictable. HIS 'SURPRISE'. Then he blinks twice and at the same time he opens and shuts his mouth. One hand hangs loosely by his side and with the other he pulls on a lock of hair. He jumps clumsily up and down a couple of times. And then I just melt because I see he is really happy.
>
> *Hilde De Clercq*

Someone with a pervasive development disorder can be mentally retarded at the same time, but this means that there is also something else wrong apart from the pervasive development disorder. The word 'pervasive' implies that someone is affected deep inside, throughout his entire being. That is the case with people with autism.

What makes our lives really meaningful is communicating with other people, understanding their behaviour, dealing with materials, situations and people in a creative way. It is precisely in these three areas that people with autism find life most difficult.

The expression 'pervasive disorder' is a much better way of explaining what is the matter with these people than is the simple word 'autism'. If people suffer from a combination of difficulties with the development of communication, social understanding and imagination, and, moreover, suffer from specific difficulties in understanding what they see and hear, the label 'autistic' in the limited sense of 'turned in on oneself' or 'aloof' is not the best definition. Their real difficulties are much broader than this single characteristic of social withdrawal.

1.3. Neither mental illness nor psychosis

It is important that autism is no longer grouped with mental illnesses or psychoses as it was in the past. In 1970 the most important international professional journal on autism was launched. Originally it was called *The Journal of Autism and Childhood Schizophrenia*. Later the title was changed into *Journal of Autism and Developmental Disorders*. Most researchers have since become convinced that the study of the connection between autism and mental illness has become less meaningful and that it is more relevant to direct future research towards the comparison between autism and other development disorders.

The term 'mental illness' implies that the first form of treatment is psychiatric; only when psychiatric treatment has proved sufficiently successful is attention given to (some special form of) upbringing and education.

In the case of pervasive development disorders, special education is the first priority for treatment. In exceptional circumstances psychiatric treatment is also necessary. With autism, this may, for example, have to do with the difficulties that high-functioning people with autism face in coming to terms with the fact that they are handicapped and with their efforts to hide this. They often try very hard but are still continually confronted with their helplessness. It would take less than this for most people to become depressed. For the treatment of their depression help can best be found with a psychiatrist who specializes in autism.

I am not arguing against medical involvement with autism. I merely want to see closer cooperation between the educational and medical sectors than we now have. We must be realistic, however: autism is not an illness. If the most valuable treatment consists of a suitable education, doctors should not necessarily be the first port of call in all circumstances.

Another important difference between a pervasive developmental disorder and mental illness concerns the ultimate goal of treatment. Someone who is mentally ill was once 'normal' so one tries to make him 'normal' again. In the case of autism one must accept that the development disorder is permanent. The aim, then, of treatment is to develop all possibilities within those parameters, in other words prepare the child for adult life so that he or she is integrated into society as much as possible (while still being protected).

It is very important that psychiatry confirms this definition of autism. Then autism will be more correctly diagnosed within the world of psychiatry and distinguished from true psychiatric disorders. In this way, the psychiatrist can help to indicate the best system of care and, as we have said, eventually provide extra support if a person with autism develops other psychiatric problems.

1.4. Unable is not the same as unwilling – there is no lack of motivation

If autism falls under the category of developmental disorders and no longer under that of mental illness, it becomes immediately clear that lack of motivation is not one of autism's fundamental problems. At one time it was thought that the poor intellectual achievements of children with autism were the result of a conscious refusal to interact socially, but as Rutter (1983) wrote:

1. If their poor intellectual achievements were the result of a lack of social motivation they would all, without exception, score at the same low level of intelligence on IQ tests. This is not the case.
2. IQ tests have the same prognostic value for autistic children (particularly those of low intelligence) as they do for normal children, both in terms of achievement at school and in terms of the level of adult independence they can hope to reach.
3. Moreover, an improvement in their 'psychological state' (for example, increased social involvement) does not lead to a higher intelligence quota.
4. A number of studies have shown that IQ scores do not depend on motivation. (Of course this does not mean that motivation cannot affect achievement, as it does for both non-handicapped and

mentally retarded children). In a number of tests, if children failed the first tasks, they were given simpler ones which they could perform better. If they answered questions correctly they were given progressively more difficult tasks until they reached their level of failure – not through a lack of motivation but because the tasks become too difficult.

5. Finally, the epileptic attacks suffered by children with autism are associated with a low IQ: one in three of the mentally retarded children with autism suffers epileptic fits as compared to one in twenty among better-functioning persons with autism. There is no way that this can be explained by a lack of social involvement or motivation.

Low IQs (60 per cent of persons with autism have IQs under 50) are not then the result of weak social motivation. Mental retardation and autism go together from the beginning. The way parents must constantly put up with ignorant reactions from those who interpret the helplessness of people with autism as unwillingness is illustrated in the following quote:

> Thomas had his set routines at school. He never played. He walked around the playground constantly holding the hand of one teacher he called 'Hand' ('Hold my hand'). If the teacher didn't have time for him she gave him a microphone which he would sit and lick constantly. At certain times of the day he wanted to hear music as well. All the school knew Thomas as 'the little boy who is always turning on the taps, who opens all the cupboards, turns all the lights on and off, spills the tortoise's food all over the floor, empties the milk cartons', etc. If you couldn't keep Thomas sitting at the table and occupied, he would behave like that. He was often a problem at home as well. For example, when we had visitors, he would start opening and closing the fridge and all the doors, he'd turn the lights on and off, empty drawers, bang on various objects, all sorts of things. We had many different reactions from visitors like 'Put him in the cellar and he'll soon listen' or 'Let me deal with him, he'll soon toe the line.' Luckily I never took any of this knowing advice.
>
> *Hilde De Clercq*

1.5 What's in a word? Labels can save lives

You must have sometimes heard it said that it doesn't make any difference whether people are called 'mentally ill' or 'mentally retarded/developmentally disabled'. After all, aren't these just words?

But there are consequences attached to these words. Because of them many adults with autism are living in psychiatric institutions under the wrong label. You will also find people who are autistic in groups of the mentally retarded who have behavioural problems. Their tragedy is that although they are suffering from the developmental disorder of autism, they are being treated for mental illness or ordinary mental retardation. This is not how it should be, but it is still the case that the quality of an autistic person's life depends less on the extent of his handicap and more on the place where he was born and whether it is a place where autism is properly understood. In this sense diagnostic labels can save lives. It makes a tremendous difference to an individual whether he is given medication or specialized education as his main form of treatment. The same is true of the care of people with autism. Are the specific needs of autistic people for specially adapted daily care and activities taken into account?

Children with autism can have behavioural problems, communication problems, and hearing problems and be mentally retarded. It is a disaster for them if they are treated in the same way as non-autistic children with behavioural or hearing problems or mental retardation. This is because the reason for their difficulties is different and a thorough understanding of autism should be the starting point for a psycho-educational approach. How a disorder is diagnosed determines the sort of help a child is given. An argument for the right diagnostic label is an argument for proper treatment.

1.6. Parents need clarity: they need an answer to their questions

A lot of well-meaning advice given to parents of children with autism creates extra burdens because professionals often do not sufficiently understand how specific the disorder of autism is. Those who do not understand this will not be able to give parents the best help.

Parents of children with autism often go from one professional to another looking for the best diagnosis, for proper understanding and for advice on how to bring up and deal with their children. If the explanations are not relevant, they look elsewhere (and sometimes even give up).

I know dozens of parents who made the diagnosis themselves. That is the wrong way round but it does not change things: ultimately, they must convince the professionals that the problem is autism rather than mental retardation or deafness. That is what happened to Mary Akerley:

> I made the diagnosis myself, thanks to an article on the front page of the *Washington Post*. The National Association of Autistic Adults and Children were holding their annual conference and the paper described the symptoms in the report. I recognised my son in the article so, dear reader, if

you're still against labels, reread the previous lines. It comes down to this: the child will be given a label sooner or later. Certainly in our case, and, in my opinion, in most cases, it's better sooner than later. Had we known at once that Ed had autism, we would have been very sad, but not nearly so unsure and afraid . . .

Imagine a similar situation. You have a dreadful headache and take a double dose of aspirin. Your headache gets better but only briefly. Finally you go to your doctor and he prescribes medicine which also only works temporarily. You go back to the doctor, he does some tests and says the blood vessels in the right side of your head have narrowed . . . You want to know why the blood vessels have narrowed. Is it a tumour or just nerves? And until you know what causes your headache you will feel very nervous, scared and unhappy.

Parents of handicapped children also want to know why. I don't mean the philosophical 'why'. That comes much later. I mean 'why' from a professional standpoint so that they are at least sure that professionals will be able to help their child. Don't forget: whether we are talking about the patient with a headache or parents with a handicapped child, we are talking about people who are frightened. Something terrible has happened to them and as long as the situation isn't taken seriously the fear will not go away. Parents cannot cope by themselves. Unless the parent happens to be a pediatrician or a psychologist himself, he or she will not have the necessary knowledge to know what to do. The parents are as helpless as the child is.

1.7. Preventing or eliminating misunderstanding with parents

I remember one French father telling me how he thought at first that his son had a mental illness: professionals had told him that his son was very intelligent, that his son found the world about him too facile, substandard, not sufficiently adapted to his 'superior' intelligence. Every now and then his son took him by the hand and pulled him to the fridge as if to say 'I want some fruit juice.' The father found this humiliating. Why did his son do this? What had he done wrong to deserve such treatment? Why was he being treated like a fool?

At first the father interpreted his son's behaviour as a character defect: he's making a fool of me. That didn't have a very positive effect on the development of a good relationship between them. Later other professionals explained that it was quite normal for a child of a certain age to take his father by the hand to show him something. It only meant that the child did not yet know how to control his environment with other forms of communication. But such behaviour usually lasts only a short time with ordinary children and parents quickly forget it. Children with autism, however, can not manage such ordinary (virtually spontaneous) development on their own; they seem to become frozen at certain stages. That is why we must reveal what they cannot see themselves, for example by leading them physically to the fridge and showing them how to open it.

When the child's father realized this the relationship changed at once. He was not dealing with a 'perverse' child after all, but one with a very specific handicap. The fact that his son took him by the hand and led him to the fridge was now seen as positive: his son was trying to communicate with him. It was on a different level (he still could not talk), but he was doing his best. And the father had also found a way to help his son.

One still encounters situations, however, in which professionals insist that you cannot do anything for a child who is not motivated. 'Le desir' is not yet there, the child does not yet 'want' to develop, we must wait for that desire before we can help. In fact, it should be clear that people must give a child with autism the 'means' to develop. If a child cannot communicate with words, it does not mean that he has no will to develop, but that words are (for the time being?) too difficult. If you give the child other more concrete means of communication, communication can exist: the child now has the means available and these stimulate the will to develop further. A child cannot want what he does not understand . . .

1.8. Seen through a professional's eye: 'Different' children need 'different' help (Mary Akerley)

There are also the professionals who (in cooperation with parents) try to 'mend' so-called 'broken' children. Like the parents, they want to know the reason for the difficulties these children have; they can only help if they understand the problem. Like the parents, they either give up or go under when they don't understand 'why'.

Young people with autism differ from other mentally handicapped people, they differ from children with psychological problems, from children with language delay, from deaf children. The new approach to autism within special education has shown that children with autism are different and thus need a different approach. Traditional 'special education' is not special enough.

The more one handicap looks like another, the more important it is to make a correct diagnosis and to use the correct label, Mary Akerley writes. Thus it is of the greatest importance that professionals understand what makes autism so special. Professional care that does not do this inevitably attracts behavioural problems without meaning to.

From theoretical understanding to educational intervention

A pervasive developmental disorder demands life-time specialized facilities for autism

It is obvious that life-long care is needed for some handicaps. To give someone with a severe mental handicap special education and then turn him out at the age of 21 saying he needs no more help is unthinkable . . . impossible. People with autism also need continuous specialized care. That, of course, implies continuity in specially provided facilities. Once one realizes this, one can understand why the American TEACCH programme serves as a model for many parents and professionals. TEACCH stands for Treatment and Education of Autistic and related Communication Handicapped Children. In the state of North Carolina, which has a population of about six million, there are six diagnostic centres specializing in autism with home training services, more than 150 classes for children and adolescents with autism, and a number of specialized living and working facilities for adults with autism. Together these facilities form their programme. The name TEACCH, then, stands for the state programme. Unfortunately, the term 'programme' is sometimes wrongly interpreted, as if it were some sort of recipe book, a 'programme' that you can simply buy and use, just like that. This would be a denial of exactly those principles of individualization which are so important for an approach to autism. If we say that TEACCH is a model for us, it is primarily because we too want continuity in specialized autism facilities, for all ages and for all levels of intelligence.

Chapter 2
The problem with meaning

1. Theoretical understanding

We have now reached the point at which we understand that autism is a developmental disorder, a pervasive disorder, and not a form of mental illness. What then is so special about this handicap? What makes a child with autism so different from other handicapped children?

1.1. Cognition. How the brain processes sensory information

Cognition is about understanding. How does someone learn to 'understand'? Children see, hear, feel and taste. What do they do with all this sensory information? They learn to perceive, to understand, to think abstractly . . . cognition deals with processes such as paying attention and remembering.

If we say that people with autism have a different cognitive style, we basically mean that their brains process information differently. They hear, feel and see, but their brains deal with this information in a different way (which is why the DSM IV definition of autism refers to 'qualitative impairments' in communication and social interaction).

Most people with autism are also mentally handicapped, but their problems with the development of communication, social behaviour and imagination cannot be explained simply by retarded development. To help someone with autism implies that you understand not only that they may be developmentally handicapped, but that they are also different in other ways.

1.2. Autism with mental handicap and autism alone: what is the difference?

At one time, people were not aware that autism and mental handicap usually go hand in hand. People would ask, is the child mentally handicapped or is he autistic? A better question would have been, is this child autistic and is he also mentally handicapped? What is the difference between autism with mental handicap and autism alone? The difference can be seen in Figure 2.1.

Here you see an illustration of the PEP test results of an autistic boy, aged 4;6 years. The PEP (Psychological-Educational Profile) examines the development of imitation, cognitive performance, verbal expression, fine and gross motor skills, perception and eye–hand coordination in children with autism between 1 and 12 years of age. It is a standardized test, which means, among other things, that the results of this test on non-handicapped children are also known. Thus we can compare the development of a child with autism with that of normal children when the test is completed.

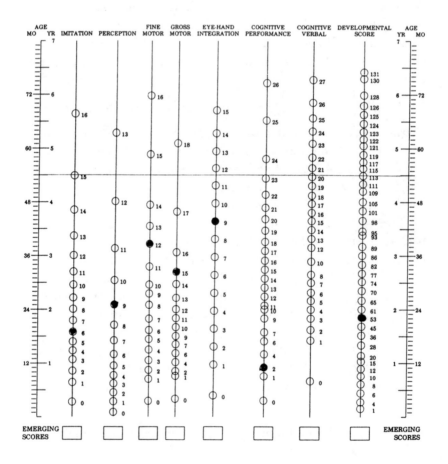

Figure 2.1 PEP test results for an autistic boy aged 4;6 years.

Johnny is aged 4;6 years: one can see that from the horizontal line between 4 and 5. On the far right one can see that he has a developmental score of 53. That means that he succeeded in doing 53 of the tasks, which corresponds to the average achievements of a normal 2-year-old. His development is much slower than expected (his developmental score should normally reach the horizontal line). Slow development shows mental handicap. Johnny can thus be defined as mentally handicapped.

If he were an 'ordinary' mentally handicapped child, you would see a more consistent learning profile: a 2-year-old's level of development on cognitive and motor skills. Thus an 'ordinary' mentally handicapped child of 4;6 years with a mental age of 2 behaves like a 2-year-old child. From the point of view of intelligence and emotional development, he IS a child of 2.

This is not so in Johnny's case. His best skill is eye–hand coordination, for which his score almost reaches the level of a 4-year-old. These strong skills of children with autism are often called 'islets of intelligence'. However, one can see that Johnny's best skill is, still, in spite of everything, at a lower level than that expected of his age group: it is simply an area about which we can say that there is a less dramatic deviation. In the area of cognitive skills Johnny is not so lucky. In terms of understanding language and speaking he has a mental age of under 6 months. Taken altogether it is an example of very uneven development, a very inconsistent profile, one which is typical of children with autism. In this case autism is coupled with mental handicap, something one can see clearly in the profile; there is a wide variance, the areas of communication and social understanding being the most deeply affected.

That is what we mean when we refer to 'qualitative impairment' of the development of communication and social interaction. The difficulties cannot be explained in terms of a lower mental age alone. Here you are facing not only a slower development, but also one that is different, indeed a different kind of cognition.

1.3. Autism and mental handicap. Realistic expectations for the future

Before we discuss the deviant cognitive style of young people with autism, it is necessary to consider the possibility of mental handicap that is also often found in children with autism. It can be a shock to parents if the original diagnosis mentions only 'autism' but does not simultaneously provide the necessary information about any mental handicap that is also present.

Most people with autism are also moderately or severely mentally handicapped (60 per cent have an IQ under 50, where 100 is considered to be an average score). It is therefore important that parents and professionals realize that even with the best programmes in the world using the most highly trained specialists in autism, mental handicap will remain. The level of mental handicap determines the level of hope and expectation one may hold out for the future (without becoming too fatalistic).

- People with mild mental handicap score between 52 and 67 on IQ tests. By 9 years of age, children with mild mental handicap have reached a level of independent functioning that a more severely retarded adult reaches only years later. For example, they can dress themselves and look after their personal hygiene. They can also be expected to communicate in complex sentences and to have reasonably good work skills. Autistic people in this group tend to have the most variable skills. Some children have special peak skills which they can later develop into means for earning a livelihood. Autistic children with musical 'peak' skills, for example might become, among other things, piano tuners. However, because of the severity of their language impairment, few autistic children achieve this level of functioning. Most autistic children function at a moderate or severe level of retardation.
- The moderately retarded score falls approximately between 36 and 51 on IQ tests. The adaptive behaviour of moderately retarded adults may include self-feeding, bathing and dressing, and communication in the form of simple conversations and limited reading. Occupation skills may be limited to routine chores. These individuals are often placed in 'trainable' classes in schools, and a minority of this group achieve independent living as adults.
- Severe mental handicap is associated with IQ scores in the 20–35 range, and independent functioning would be expected only in limited areas, such as washing the face and hands or running simple errands. Social and communication skills are greatly limited, and vocational activity requires careful supervision.
- Those with IQ levels of 19 or below are considered profoundly retarded. Their numbers are relatively small, but their handicap is so pervasive that it makes them totally dependent in most areas of functioning.

Schopler, E., Reichler, R. and Lansing, M.,
Teaching Strategies for Parents and
Professionals. Austin, Pro-Ed, 1980.

Above, we have given a short overview of the future prospects for people with mental handicap. This list is not, of course, absolute, but it offers a developmental outline that can be used as a realistic guide. For people with autism, calculating a similar independence level will be more difficult in terms of the future because of the extra handicap (difficulties with communication, social understanding and imagination) that autism brings. This is why it is important to understand how the combination of disorders affects children with autism.

1.4. Autism in combination with other handicaps. Autism is the proper starting point for education

Even when other disorders are present (mental handicap, deafness, blindness, etc.), it is still necessary to think first in terms of autism when planning education. It is obvious that problems which involve interpreting and understanding the meaning of objects, events and people must be attended to first.

Mental handicap is a problem mainly of backwardness; being blind, deaf or having another sensory handicap does not affect one's ability to enjoy a meaningful life. However, for those with autism, life is naturally chaotic; situations seem to be governed by chance. The problem of interpreting and understanding must be treated first; the other problems come later. This explains why mentally handicapped children with autism, as well as deaf or blind children with autism, also benefit from an autism class, as it first treats the problem they have with meaning.

1.5 Autism without mental handicap? Yes and no

Twenty per cent of people with autism are considered to have an average or above average IQ. What does this mean? A government bureaucrat who is not familiar with the problem will no doubt find it difficult to understand that someone who has an average or above average IQ still needs special education.

We have already explained that the word 'autism' is not the best term to describe problems with interpreting and understanding the meaning of things. The expression 'pervasive developmental disorder' is closer. 'Average' intelligence and 'above average' intelligence also do not adequately describe such people because those with autism and above average intelligence are often seriously handicapped socially.

It is worthwhile spending a little time looking at what we mean by 'intelligence'. What is intelligence? People will sometimes scornfully say that intelligence is what is measured by intelligence tests. Binet's original aim was not to measure individual differences among the average population but to spot children who had learning delays (or a mental handicap) that were not due to environmental disadvantage alone.

The creators of intelligence tests reason as follows: if we use toys or developmental materials that are most often found in the homes of the higher social classes and not found in the others, children from wealthier backgrounds automatically have an advantage over children from less-privileged backgrounds, something we want to avoid. In order not to use materials, ask questions and analyse situations that are particular only to certain social classes, we must avoid real-life situations, thereby formulating tests that are not taken from real life.

This is what Uta Frith called the difference between 'test' intelligence and 'world' intelligence (intelligence used for taking tests and intelligence used in daily life, sometimes called 'common sense'). She gives the example of Brazilian street children who cannot do a sum on paper (a form of abstract intelligence) but who can deal easily with money because they sell bananas to tourists (a form of 'applied', practical intelligence).

You see the opposite in high-functioning individuals with autism. They can do complicated sums on paper and in their heads, but cannot deal properly with money in daily life (think of the main character in the film *Rain Man*). They lack 'common sense'. They are reasonably intelligent in an abstract way but not in a practical way. In this sense you might call them socially handicapped.

> Charles is in his first year at university, studying history. Family trees have always been his hobby. He knows whole books off by heart, which impresses his fellow students – perhaps more so because of his helplessness in other areas. They cannot figure him out. Charles is a wonder boy, but have you ever seen him order a sandwich? He doesn't like butter, but instead of ordering a sandwich without butter, he just orders the first thing that comes into his head. If is a sandwich with butter, he pays for it, goes outside and throws it into the first dustbin he comes to. He has never learned to ask for 'a sandwich without butter.'

1.6. Cognitive experiments with children with autism

Those who want to help people with autism need to understand not only their slower development, but also their 'unusual' development and their 'qualitative' impairments. How are we to understand these unusual problems, the problems of interpreting and understanding?

The English researchers Hermelin and O'Connor first published their important discoveries in 1970 in the book *Psychological Experiments with Autistic Children*. Their research was both simple and fascinating. They asked three groups of children with the same mental age (children with autism, ordinary children and mentally handicapped children without autism) to complete a number of tasks. They decided to select autistic children without mental handicap as this gave them the best chance to get a picture of pure autism, that is, one not complicated by an associated mental retardation. One would normally expect in such experiments that children of the same mental age would have similar levels of achievement. In fact they discovered that children with autism were (in spite of their similar developmental age) completely at a loss over certain tasks that the other groups were able to do. This suggested that they had found something typical of autism. They thus had an hypothesis and could set up similar experiments. If all the experiments confirmed the original hypothesis, this would be considered scientific proof of it. (The science philosopher Karl Popper says that the humanities can only be called 'scientific' if they formulate assumptions that can be proved or disproved through experimentation. The psychoanalytical approach to autism has no such scientific status; it is a theory that one either does or does not believe – it cannot be proved or disproved by scientific experiments. The theory may be interesting but it is not scientific.)

1.7. Adding meaning to perceptions: a limited ability to interpret and understand

Hermelin wrote:

> This cognitive pathology seems to consist largely of an inability to reduce information through the appropriate extraction of crucial features such as rules and redundancies. The impairment in these processes imposes well-remembered, stereotyped and restricted behaviour patterns, which become increasingly inappropriate as the requirements for complex, flexible codes increase. It is in the areas of language development and social interaction, which are governed by such complex and flexible rules, that the autistic child's cognitive impairment becomes most evident.

For example, in one experiment the verbal memory of the three groups of children was examined. What follows is a simplified description that retains the spirit of the experiment. The details can be read in the original publication listed in the bibliography. In the first phase the children were asked to memorize as many words as possible from an arbitrary list (for example, 'window – apple – overhead projector – water – book – perhaps – run'). The three groups achieved equally well, as would be expected of children with the same mental age.

In the second phase of the experiment, words were now presented in a meaningful context: meaning became part of the equation (for example apple – grape – grapefruit – lemon – pear – car – boat – aeroplane). If we heard such a list we might immediately react by thinking; 'I know. It's about fruit and transport. From the moment our perceptions are linked to content meaning, our memories work more efficiently: adding meaning helps us to organize our lives. In that test the achievements of the normal and mentally handicapped children increased while the achievements of the children with autism, in spite of the same level of intelligence, stayed at the previous level: adding meaning to perception helped them much less. Anyone who thinks deeply about this experiment and attempts to understand what goes on in the mind of a child with autism draws some intriguing conclusions.

If someone with autism has as much of a problem with 'meaning' in his daily life as he did in this experiment, he will be rather isolated in a world where meaning is commonly found through communication and social behaviour. He will then be much more dependent on perceptual information than his mental age would suggest.

The psychologist Jerome Bruner examined the cognitive development of ordinary children and was impressed by their talent to go beyond the merely perceptual (the title of one of his books is *Beyond the Information Given*). Ordinary children see and hear things that are not readily apparent. In other words they have the talent to infer and add meaning to their perceptions.

We see that, from birth, as they develop the means of communication, children intuitively realize that human sounds are more important than other sounds. As time goes by, even without lessons, they begin to understand human language and learn to talk. An impressive achievement if we think what an effort it costs us as adults (when the brain is so much less flexible) to learn a new language. Children thus learn to add meaning to the perception of sound. They come to understand abstractions: the sound 'glass' has only an arbitrary relationship to the object 'glass'. In other languages people use other sounds for it: '*verre*', '*vaso*', '*bicchiere*'.

Sometimes we don't stop to think that it is also necessary to add meaning to social behaviour in order to understand it. The ability to understand social behaviour apparently lies deeply embedded in our brains and most handicapped people keep their social intuition relatively intact. In spite of their handicaps, deaf, blind, mentally handicapped and dysphasic people have no particular problems understanding social behaviour or adding meaning to social perceptions. They can understand the expression of emotions: an aphasic child lets himself be cuddled, a deaf child understands the meaning of his mother's smile.

How different this can be with autism. Think of *Rain Man* and the scene in the lift where his brother's girlfriend, who feels sympathy for him, asks him if a woman has ever kissed him. Does he know what it feels like to be kissed? She kisses him and asks him tenderly what it felt like. 'Wet', says Rain Man.

He is right. Looked at from the point of view of pure perception, a kiss is wet. His difficulty is understanding the emotion behind the wetness, adding meaning to the literal perception. This helps us to understand the deep sadness of parents who feel rejected by their child with autism. For example, at one point when it all becomes too much for her, a mother collapsed and cried and cried and cried. John, her son, who had watched the whole thing, roared with laughter. 'He was laughing at me . . . ' In fact the laughter was caused by something else. From his particular perspective the tears were a funny sight. He'd only seen water flowing from taps and now water was coming from someone's eyes: a human tap?

Professionals are also sometimes upset by this and for the same reasons. They invest emotion in the children in their care and, like the parents, often feel rejected. That is why it is important to remember that people with autism have particular difficulty 'reading' faces and the emotions behind the perceptions. If you do not recognize these emotions it is difficult to take them into account. Children with autism, in contrast to ordinary children, may not always have the talent to go beyond the pure information given. Ina van Berckelaer calls this 'living to the letter'.

Ordinary children develop social intuition from a very early age and quickly come to prefer the human race to objects. As they grow up they become more and more interested in human life around them. They also grow to understand more about it. We can see this through their symbolic play as they begin to express the fact that human behaviour is meaningful to them: they pretend to feed their doll, they put it to bed, sit it on a chair, etc.

The development of the imagination (adding meaning to perception) and social behaviour is very different in children with autism. If they are invited to play and to 'pretend', they much prefer to look for activities focusing on pure perception, such as piling up objects or putting them in rows. The lack of symbolic play shows us how little they have understood of the behaviour of their parents and siblings. (It now seems incredible that people once interpreted the asymbolic behaviour of children with autism in a highly symbolic way. If they slammed a toy cow on the table, it was seen as an expression of aggression against the mother figure).

The different cognitive style of people with autism can be summed up as follows. Everywhere in the world children are born with a biologically programmed talent to add meaning to perceptions with a minimum of social stimulation only. Thanks to this talent they intuitively prefer human sounds; in due course they analyse and understand human communication and eventually they themselves communicate. With this same talent they also succeed first in understanding human behaviour and then, in keeping with this understanding, in behaving in a socially acceptable manner. It is exactly this inborn, biological talent that is affected in people with autism. The talent is not 'absent' but it is disturbed. Many people with autism do, in fact, understand certain meanings, expressed through communication, social behaviour and imagination. The difficulties they have with adding meaning may be on a higher level.

1.8. A limited ability to interpret gestures

A new series of cognitive experiments confirmed these difficulties with interpretation. These experiments were set up in the same way as the previous one: the achievements of three groups of children were measured: one group was autistic, one mentally handicapped and a third group consisted of ordinary children, all with a mental age of 5 (Attwood et al., 1986).

The researchers found that children with autism used 'instrumental' gestures as often as did the other two groups. Such gestures are very 'iconic' (there is a visible connection between the picture and its meaning) [Figure 2.2]. In other words, meaning does not really have to be 'inferred' from it. The meaning of gestures speaks for itself. This is true of the gesture 'go away': it speaks for itself. The meaning is found in the extension of the perception itself, it is not detached from it.

Expressive gestures

Instrumental gestures

Figure 2.2

However, when the second series, 'expressive gestures', were tested, researchers discovered that children with autism did not use them at all, although ordinary children and especially those with Down syndrome, had no particular difficulties with them. They concluded that the difference between these two kinds of gesture must lie in their subtlety. One cannot see the effect of 'expressive' gestures as directly; they are used to convey complex emotions and states of mind.

Yet we might also interpret the findings in a different way. 'Expressive gestures' are much more difficult to identify for children who find it hard to understand things beyond their literal sense. Look, for example, at the gesture 'we are two close friends'. An arm around the shoulders is a very arbitrary gesture, the meaning is not clear in a purely visual sense; it is detached from the image and must be inferred from it. The group of mentally handicapped children and the group of normal children 'read' the meaning with little difficulty, but the group of children with autism failed completely. If one could enter their minds, one would understand why this sort of gesture causes problems for them. If the gesture is regarded strictly in its literal sense, all one sees is the circular movement of the arm. Why should this gesture mean 'comfort' in one context, while the same circular movement can mean 'cleaning' in another – this is the way I polish the table?

Finally, an important note. All these gestures that caused problems for children with autism were gestures that expressed feelings. This leads us to suspect that even though they have the same mental age – 5 years – as the other children in the experiment, children with autism have specific difficulties in understanding many human feelings. Indeed, if they sometimes seem unfeeling to us, it is part of their cognitive disability.

1.9. Understanding human emotional utterances

In another experiment (Baron-Cohen *et al.*, 1985) three groups of children had to put the pictures of a story in the right order (Figure 2.3).

In the 'mechanical' and the 'behavioural' stories the children with autism did not seem to have particular difficulties in comparison with other children of the same mental age. Mechanical and behavioural stories can be understood without referring to mental states. When a state of mind ('surprise') has to be attributed to a character, as in the mentalistic story, the children with autism had severe difficulties. Ordinary children and those with Down syndrome with a lower mental age performed better than did the children with autism. This is what experimenters found, but the findings might also be interpreted in a wider sense.

What can we see in these pictures? The boy puts a cake in the box, he goes out to play, 'a bad lady' eats the cake, the boy is very surprised when he finds the box empty. The problem? It is the open mouth. Feelings are harder to understand, and if these feelings are portrayed in an abstract manner it becomes completely impossible. An open mouth is not 'iconic' enough: there is no literal connection

A mechanical story

A behavioural story

A 'mentalistic' story

Figure 2.3 Three types of picture story

between the symbol and the meaning. An open mouth can mean many different things. For example, I've just eaten too many chillies, I want to go to sleep, I'm so hungry. And now, also, 'surprise'. (And who wouldn't be surprised in a world he did not understand, where everything is difficult. In fact, one is continually surprised when things are so unpredictable and incomprehensible.)

'Difficulty adding meaning to perception' says something essential about this 'different cognitive style', which we must take into account if we want to help people with autism. This different cognitive style can be found in the main characteristics of the scientific definition of autism, namely the qualitative impairments in communication, social interaction and limited stereotyped behaviour and interests (which are often the result of a qualitative impairment in the development of 'imagination').

2. From theoretical understanding to educational intervention. Interpreting the world in a different way.

If you cannot build up a positive atmosphere for education, it is better not to start. Nevertheless, it is not easy to work out a positive approach for people who are so different. Imagination, intelligence, intuition and love are all very important as investments, but with autism you also need professional knowledge.

Understanding 'beyond the literal perception' in the main problem of autism:

> Because life is such a confusing mass of sounds and sights it really helps an autistic person if he can get order into his life. It is important that the need for consistency mentioned earlier is maintained throughout each day as well as every day. This might be boring for most people but it is one of the few things that can actually relieve suffering a little. For me, it is essential to have set times and places for everything. Parents could help their children to feel safer but they would probably find their own life very dull. A problem exists: if I am going to get better I have got to let things change. There seems to be a trade off between keeping the order the same to minimize fear and changing things to progress. I would suggest that the ordinary day-to-day tasks, like having a bath, eating meals, washing hands and brushing teeth, should all be done at the same times and that a child should have a period of listening to music every day at the same time. There will then be some order and new things can be introduced in between.
>
> *Therese Joliffe et al., 1992*

2.1. Objects as comprehensible communication?

Many people with autism do not experience the coherence of things; they see few logical connections and have the impression that most of their life is dictated by chance, the unexpected, by things they cannot get a grip on. Those living in the midst of such confusion need something to hold onto, 'branches' to clutch at. Our usual verbal explanations of how and when specific happenings will take place, of the whys and wherefores are insufficient.

People who are so different from us must be approached in a different way. Isn't 'perception' their strong point? Would it not then be possible to use perception to compensate for their difficulties in comprehension, to replace the abstract with the concrete? In this way, by playing to their interests and strengths, they will become motivated more quickly. Blind people learn to read through touch. Is there not also a sort of 'Braille' for people with autism? As their cognitive style is so rigid, as they think with so little flexibility, perhaps this can be used to their advantage. If words say so little to them, can objects not speak more clearly?

On the language of the red sweater

Steven has been on holiday in the mountains with his parents and had a wonderful time. He was completely fascinated with the snow, the ice and the sun, which reflected all that white. Every day for a week, he wore a thick red sweater. That was 2 months ago. Today his mother dressed him in his red sweater again. She did not understand at first why Steven beamed with joy, but for Steven it was a sign that he was off again to the snow and the mountains. He was nervous all day because they still hadn't set off on their journey and in the evening, when they were still at home he threw a huge tantrum.

Another example. On the language of the straw bag

In contrast to many children with autism who dislike crowds, Mary enjoys going to the supermarket. Her mother always follows the same route with the trolley, she always buys a bar of chocolate at the check-out and she always takes her straw bag with her when she goes. Her mother tells the story:

> One Sunday morning I showed Mary the car keys: we're going out. Mary was very quiet until I took the left turn two miles down the road. All of a sudden she had a terrible tantrum in the car. I stopped and looked around. What was the matter? Then I saw that my straw bag was in the car. When she had seen the straw bag, Mary had, of course, thought that we were going to the supermarket and was pleased. At first the road to the super-market is the same as the one to my mother's but where I turned left, you turn right for the supermarket. That was when the tantrum began.

Such anecdotes show how people with autism try to make sense of life in their own way. If this is impossible via abstract words and under-standing, they do it through concrete perceptual associations. We will try to use this inflexibility of 'thought', these concrete associations, to their advantage. We will make a strength out of their weakness.

In the classroom, for example, the teacher will show a box every time the children have to go to work. After a few times, Mary will know that it is time to go to the work table. She will take the box and put it in a large box in the work corner. She understands. For those who have such difficulty understanding the abstract, we show the concrete. Instead of waiting (uselessly) for years for a person with a pervasive development disorder to adapt to a much too difficult envi-ronment ('He's not ready for school'), we adapt his environment.

2.2. The strong must adapt: a matter of politeness

A person with autism suffers from the lack of meaning in his life. Therefore, help with this should be the first priority. Those who do not find real security will expend a lot of energy trying to find it. In the meantime they will not be able to enjoy the simpler things in life.

It is the same for us ordinary people. Just imagine that you are invited to a 3-day conference in Bulgaria. It goes without saying that you don't speak Bulgarian, so you will have an immediate problem of communication. Moreover, you have heard that Bulgarians nod their heads up and down when they mean no, and shake their head from side to side when they mean yes. The world is turned upside down. You are on tenterhooks and extra nervous because you think, if that is the case, there will be other social conventions that are also different. You will be at a social disadvantage in Bulgaria.

At last you arrive at Sofia airport for the 3-day conference where you are expected to give a talk. Try to think what your first questions would be, taking into account your communication and social problems. They would probably concern details of your stay. The first questions would most likely be about the place: 'where' questions – where is the conference to be held, where is the conference room, where am I to sleep, where can I get something to eat? When you have answers to these questions, you will feel calmer. Children with autism need that same predictability. It makes them calmer if they can make firm associations between activities and places.

The second list of questions will be about the organization of time: 'when' questions. The programme will answer the questions of when the lectures will start, how long they will last and also when you give your lecture, when there will be a break and when you eat. When you've had all these answers, you'll feel even calmer. Everyone wants predictability in their lives.

You also think it is most natural thing in the world that the Bulgarians answer you in a way that you (with your communication and social handicap) understand: it is a simple matter of good manners. The same goes for people with autism, except that their communication and social difficulties are much more severe. They can only adapt to us with great difficulty. If we invite them to join our living groups or our classes, they are our 'guests', so we must be their interpreters. We must communicate the 'where' and 'when' information in a way that they will understand. This way we make their lives more predictable. This should not seem like a big deal: it is a simple matter of politeness.

Through their politeness the Bulgarians make us more independent in their country; through our politeness we can make autistic people more independent.

2.3. Set locations. 'Where' questions. On the organization of a class or living group

We eat in the dining room, sleep in the bedroom, wash in the bathroom. It seems logical enough: for every activity there is a special room provided. Most houses have such natural divisions. We associate certain behaviour with certain places. We do not (usually) sleep in the dining room, we do not (usually) eat in the bedroom. If we make an exception, we know that it is an exception. Nevertheless, parents trying to provide their children with some stability tell us that in fact they themselves are less predictable than they thought. Some days they dress their children in the bathroom, other days in the bedroom, still other days in the living room or kitchen. For some children this is very difficult – especially for those who want to climb the curtains instead of a climbing frame, jump on the bed instead of a trampoline. They have difficulty understanding the purpose of rooms, the behaviour that goes with the place.

In the average classroom this is even more difficult than at home. After all, how many classrooms have a workroom, a playroom and dining room? This means you must create areas in the classroom for different functions so that the pupils will have a predictable environment: this corner is for working, this one is for playing, this one for eating. When organizing the classroom you must take into account the various activities of the class: How many are there? Is it possible to create a separate space for each? To eat, play board games and then work at the same table can seem too unpredictable and therefore chaotic. It confuses the usual pattern of expectations and results in behavioural problems.

> As always at school, I felt a certain sense of security when I was in class. Any other place, however – the cafeteria, the playground, the halls – was a nightmare. I had no idea how to relate to the kids and I spent my time fearing them. I couldn't understand why they behaved as they did or what their behaviour meant.
>
> *Sean Barron, 1992*

Every class has a minimum of three different sorts of activity: you study here, so you need a work corner. You play here, so you need a

free-time corner. You eat here and learn to do the washing up, so you
need an eating corner.

Sometimes people ask why you need an eating corner in an
autism classroom. Why don't they eat with the other children? Experience has shown that children remain calm in a well-organized
autism class, but may lose this tranquillity if during lunch or playtime
they have to be with the other 'unpredictable' children. Of course,
they should learn to eat and play with other children, but it should
happen when they are ready for it. One does better at first to give
them maximum protection. After that one can think about 'integration'.

The same principles of 'spatial planning' can also be applied to
furnishing the space for 'practical training'. Setting up practical
training sessions is like setting up a new classroom. During practical
training periods teachers and other professionals learn how to create
predictability in space and time for their pupils. In the following we
change the emphasis from educating children to training the professionals. I will explain the organization of such training periods as a
source of inspiration for professionals who will create a learning or
living environment adapted to people with autism. A practical training session (based on a TEACCH model) is a course for about 20
trainees studying autism who have first followed a theoretical course
and now over the period of a week, will put theory into practice
working with actual children, adolescents and adults with autism.
There are at least five teachers-trainers responsible for each session.
Each of these teachers is responsible for one particular child, adolescent or adult with autism for the entire week. The trainees are
divided into five groups of four each (under the supervision of one
teacher-trainer). Each day they will work with a different pupil with
autism so that by the end of the week they will have gained experience with pupils of various ages and levels of intelligence.

The training situation includes all the ingredients that can lead to
behaviour problems. 'People with autism don't like changes or new
things . . .' but what do you see during such a training session? Five
people with autism who don't (or hardly) know each other are
brought together. They don't know the five teachers. For a whole
week, they will be with 20 trainees whom they don't know either.
They don't know the building where the training takes place. They
don't know the new routines. The tasks they will complete will be
new to them. In spite of this there are few behaviour problems.
People sometimes ask if we 'select' our pupils, taking only those with
few behavioural problems: the answer is no, we do not. However, we

do ask that pupils with serious problems with 'proximity' do not take part in the training sessions. These pupils can be integrated into an autism class, but during a training session they would be confronted with the proximity of far too many new people. You would be subjecting such a pupil to a very frustrating week with 30 adults around him.

The secret of success is simple: it is a combination of making the environment predictable, of routines, and combining these with tasks with which the pupils can cope or nearly cope.

2.4 Adapting space

Setting up a space for the practical training session is very similar to setting up a new autism class or living group. Teachers there use similar reasoning, and they usually start out with as few basic facts as we do.

Here is an example. In one particular training session our pupils with autism were: Luke, aged 5; Max, aged 10; Catherine, aged 15; Paul, aged 21; and Peter, aged 25. We asked for some elementary information beforehand on communication, the ability to cope, work skills, work behaviour, free-time skills and social skills. We asked if certain skills had been 'achieved', were 'emerging' or had 'failed' to be achieved. Sometimes these levels were creatively interpreted. One girl was said to be able to set the table, but on Monday, the first day of the training, we saw that she could only put an object on the table with help. One adult, who, according to his file, worked in the library, could only stamp envelopes under physical guidance.

These comments only serve to point out that one does what one can; everything is prepared as well as possible, in the same way that a class or living group is organized. However, only in practice can we see if it will work. The pupils with autism soon show by their behaviour whether the tasks are within their grasp or not. Every educational process is one of constant evaluation. We often need to begin altering tasks from the first day of the training session. We first saw the training space on Saturday morning. At one end the room had windows from floor to ceiling, which looked out onto the garden. It was not logical to use it as a work space: it would be the free-time area and it would be as large as possible. On the other side of the room there was only a wall, with no doors or windows. This would become the work corner. Next to the free-time area we would set up the eating area. That was the first rough division.

Let us now look more closely at the work space. What did we have in mind when we allotted our pupils their places. Let us consider first our efforts to make them as independent as possible. That is, after all, the most important motivation for dividing up this space.

Luke, our youngest, at 5 years was, according to the report, a veritable dynamo. He had not yet developed the habit of sitting still at a table. He still did not understand that there were separate places for work (where you did what you were asked) and free time (where you could do more or less what you wanted). His attention wandered. He would be put into a kind of 'box', screened on both sides and behind. He had to learn to pay attention to the most important items during the work times – his own task. Others had to be kept out of his field of vision. He would find it difficult to concentrate and sort out the important from the unimportant, even in this strictly adapted situation. Moreover, his work sessions would probably be very short and he would move over to the free-time area much more often than the others. His work corner was thus well screened but near the free-time area which was nevertheless outside his line of vision because of its association with 'play behaviour'.

We are often asked about these 'boxes'. The box question seems to have replaced the question that used to come up constantly 10 years ago about the 'limited use of language'. Then people found it strange that teachers talked so little and that they often directed only key words to the poor children with autism. This does indeed sound militaristic and cold. No doubt the old idea of the 'cold mother' had something to do with it. That was before people realized that children with autism have severe communication problems. Now it is normal for professionals not to encourage logorrhoea (verbal diarrhoea). As far as the 'boxes' go, it is important to understand that this has nothing to do with 'locking children up' but rather with the difficulty people with autism have in paying attention to the relevant stimuli.

The screened-off space is a means to free children from disturbances in their concentration. It is not an end in itself; it is a starting point. Look at the following drawings carefully before you read the explanation. I think you will then better understand the importance of correctly adapting the surroundings. (Note: you can see that this classroom is arranged very differently from the traditional classroom. The pupils all have tables for independent work. They are unable to follow instructions intended for the entire group.)

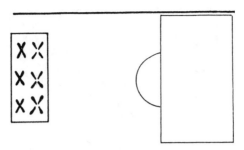

Figure 2.4

In Figure 2.4 you see the pupil sitting as we like to see him best: looking into the open space and busy at his work. His shelf is a few metres behind him. Here he collects and stores his work. He makes the move from his work table to the shelf by himself.

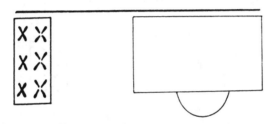

Figure 2.5

The pupil in Figure 2.5 is sitting in front of a wall, a few metres away from his work shelf to his left. He has no problem bridging the gap between the work table and the shelf. He takes out and puts his work back himself.

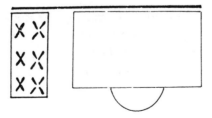

Figure 2.6

In Figure 2.6 you can see that the pupil is less independent. He takes his tasks from his work rack to the left and stores them back to the left without having to get up. He immediately becomes confused if he leaves his work table.

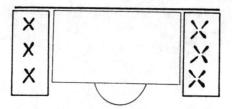

Figure 2.7

This pupil in Figure 2.7 is used to working from left to right. Taking work from the left and storing it there is too much for him. He would have to organize himself too much. Working from left to right has become automatic for him, and this has greatly improved his independence. He is not ready yet to move to the next stage. That will (maybe) come later.

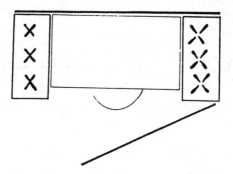

Figure 2.8

The next pupil in Figure 2.8, works in the same way as the last one but he needs screening behind him because he is immediately distracted if someone enters the classroom or if another pupil walks past him on the way to the free-time area.

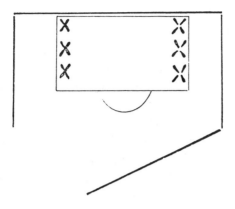

Figure 2.9

Luke sits in a 'box' as in Figure 2.9. He has not yet reached the stage of independence that would allow him to take his tasks from the shelf on the right and store them on the left. Everything still has to be done with physical supervision. The teacher has put three tasks on the table and will hand them to him one at a time. When they are completed the teacher will help him to put them away at the right.

There is a long road to follow before we will see Luke sitting as in Figure 2.4. It is probably necessary to see the final goal to understand the meaning of the initial screening off. It entails working in small steps. If you eventually want to move 5 metres you must start with millimetres.

Peter (aged 25) is also easily distracted. He is at a level equivalent to the pupil in Figure 2.6. If he is confused, he quickly develops behaviour problems. He is easily confused by moves. He does not remember what is expected of him once he is on his way. He forgets what he is doing. His lack of confidence and his feelings of failure make him very nervous. Peter lives at home with his parents. No institution will take him because of his behaviour problems. His parents do not want him in a traditional psychiatric institution where he is treated as mentally ill instead of developmentally disabled. However, if you try to adapt yourself to him, offer him predictability and give him tasks at his level, he is really a good fellow. If he has problems he will warn you. He will bang his hand on the table and say, 'You hit'. In the same situation (when things are not so bad) he may say, 'You want to go home.'

Catherine (aged 15) is a special case. Well, they all are, but Catherine
... talks. Sometimes she talks a lot. The problem is that many of those
around her think that she understands everything she says and consider
her a 'high-functioning' individual with autism because she talks. Yet in
spite of this she has great difficulty organising her behaviour and she is
very dependent. We know this because Catherine has taken part in a
previous training session. We also know before we start that our
students will ask many questions about the fact that Catherine's work
corner is also well protected. She will take tasks from the left and also
store them there (as in Figure 2.5), but there will be a screen behind her.
She is easily distracted and then quickly develops behaviour problems.

Max (aged 10) and Paul (aged 21) have better work behaviour. We
put them in a more open space, opposite each other as shown in
Figure 2.10. Max is slightly verbal; he talks very softly and hoarsely.
In unadapted situations he acts chaotically, nodding his head wildly.

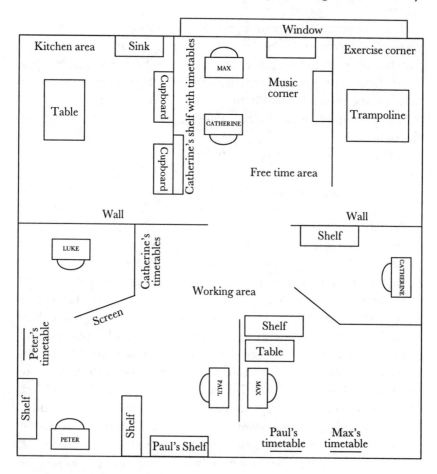

Figure 2.10 Training area

However, as soon as he is sitting in his work corner, with a clearly visualized explanation (with drawings), he perks up. Then he seems almost normal.

We have had Paul on our courses for 3 years. At the beginning he was declared uneducable. He has been living with his parents for the last 2 years: he was too difficult for the majority of institutions. He is a bit like Peter: a severely handicapped adult with autism who cooperates well if everything is made clear to him and if the tasks are ones he is capable of. But if the tasks are too confused or at too high a level – watch out!

In Figure 2.10 you can see how we installed the work corner. We see whether we are right or not, whether this is the best set-up, only when it is put into practice. We do our best; the rest is evaluation. During the training sessions the plan sometimes has to be drastically altered. That is not seen as a set-back: it is normal.

During this training session the free-time area needed the most adapting. In the drawing you see that it is well-defined, with Swedish benches and furniture. The borders between the free-time area, the eating corner and the work corner are visually well-defined and even divided up by objects. We had decided to install a number of smaller corners in the free time area: a sitting corner for Paul, because he likes listening to music, and a quiet place to do puzzles or leaf through a magazine.

On Monday we realized that the free-time area had to be more defined, particularly for Peter and Luke, but also for Catherine who seems to have difficulty with this unstructured situation. If we are not careful, overactive Luke bumps into Peter, who finds it important to be left alone. This could result in an 'accident'. Peter does not understand why Luke bumps into him, and helpless little Luke might even be slapped. Prevention is better than cure. And then there's Catherine, who is unable to develop any initiative of her own in the free-time area. She wanders aimlessly around and (perhaps out of boredom, through lack of any alternative) kicks out at anyone nearby who seems weaker than she is. We will put another table with a rack for her in this space so that she does not always have to take the initiative herself as it is clearly too difficult. One part of 'free time' will also be adapted with a free-time schedule. It must be understood that we are talking about both predictability and the prevention of behavioural problems.

One of the most important educational strategies in dealing with behaviour problems is to adapt the environment. This must be as individualized as possible.

2.5. Experiencing time: creating a visible time path. Courses in time management

> Life is such a struggle; indecision over things that other people refer to as trivial results in an awful lot of inner distress. For instance, if somebody at home says 'We may go shopping tomorrow' or if somebody says 'We will see what happens', they do not seem to realize that the uncertainty causes a lot of inner distress and that I constantly labour, in a cognitive sense, over what may or may not occur. The indecision over events extends to indecision over other things, such as where objects are to be put or found and over what people are expecting from me.
>
> It is the confusion that results from not being able to understand the world around me which I think causes all the fear. This fear then brings a need to withdraw. Anything which helps reduce the confusion (and a few people can actually be useful here) has the effort of reducing the fear and ultimately reduces the isolation and despair, thus making life a bit more bearable to live in. If only other people could experience what autism is like just for a few minutes, they might then know how to help.

> *Therese Joliffe et al., 1992*

In the definition of autism we hear of qualitative impairments in the development of social interaction, communication and imagination. Personally, I would like to add 'the experience of time'. People with autism have difficulty understanding abstract aspects of our social interaction, of our communication. They have difficulty 'going beyond the information', 'seeing beyond the literal'. So how can they understand what 'invisible time' is? People with autism have serious and understandable difficulties with this which cannot be explained only by a lower level of development.

Look at us: what do we do to control time? We make time 'visible' by means of diaries, calendars, clocks and watches. By making time visible and measurable, we succeed more easily in bringing it under control. In certain companies, courses in 'time management' are organized in an effort to use time more efficiently. I like the term 'time management' when I think about children with autism: they too must learn to manage time. Many behaviour problems are connected with their inability to do this.

The quoted experience above reveals the amount of fear and panic that are connected to the insecurity of not knowing what will happen. In this case it concerns an exceptionally well-functioning adult with autism. A high-functioning boy who used to be one of our pupils was so verbal that he himself was capable of putting into words his feelings about the help offered by visual aids in the course (daily timetables, work schedules, task organization, etc.):

> I think it's a pity that my teacher doesn't follow the course herself. The schedules make my life easier. They don't want to use the schedules in my ordinary class.
>
> *Jonathan, age 12*

If high-functioning individuals with autism have this sort of problem, we can only assume that it is just as acute for lower-functioning individuals, although they find it more difficult to express. Just look at the number of parents who complain that their children with autism cannot wait for things.

> If he smells food, he wants to eat it – immediately – even if the meat has just been put into the pan. If you explain to him that he has to wait, he throws a tantrum.

A problem of time management. How can children with autism cope with something as abstract as 'duration'? We can help them by making duration concrete, audible, visible. A kitchen timer can work wonders. How long does a child have to wait in the living room before it is time to eat? Until he hears the kitchen timer. Mary has problems moving from one situation to another. Wherever she is, she wants to stay. A move that has not previously been announced is sure to result in a tantrum. We can help her by letting her look at the kitchen timer. Then she can prepare herself for the change. In 3 minutes, the alarm will go off. Now she is prepared. How long must a child stay in the free-time area? He listens to four songs on the cassettes. When the music stops, it is time to go to work. We make time visible with our watches. Children with autism can look at an egg timer. When the sand has run out, it is time . . . .

The father of one child with autism converted music into a strip of light. At the beginning of playtime you can hear music and the strip is very long. As time goes by, the strip of light becomes shorter. This is a sort of autism-watch.

Children can also learn the sequence of activities via pictures or other symbols. Dinner? No, not yet. Look, the card says that you first must go to the free-time area. The card with dinner comes after that.

One of their problems is that if we say 'no', that 'no' sounds so final. The children cannot understand that what is 'no' now, can be 'yes' later. A card that comes a little later in the daily timetable will make that later 'yes' visible, the 'no' only temporary.

2.6. When do we do this? When do we do that? Making the course of the day visible

Like us, people with autism need a schedule, a schedule that they can make themselves or, if that is too difficult, one made by someone else for them.

A schedule or daily timetable is too much for many: they cannot predict or digest that much time. In the beginning a daily timetable is perhaps simply learning to recognize the predictable sequence of two activities, one following the other. To learn to recognize an order in things. To learn to 'see' that their lives are not dictated by chance.

Which symbols can one use for this? (see Figures 3.2 and 3.3 p.75,76). The written word is far too abstract for many of them and pictures can be too flat (two dimensions to depict three-dimensional objects or activities). When necessary one can use something three-dimensional: an object that will be used in the next activity, for example, a plate to eat from, a screw to work with, a ball to play with. This is the way in which a child learns that the world is predictable: a plate announces lunch time, a ball announces playtime.

Don't forget that a child with autism will need physical guidance at the beginning of this learning process, just as he needs physical guidance with so many other learning processes. You help him take the plate to the table, you help him take the ball to the free-time area. He will only understand the connection later. If you just put a ball or plate within his field of vision and wait until he understands what you want, you'll have to do a lot of waiting and waste a lot of time. That may not be important as far as your time is concerned, but it is for the child who will be without that new insight that much longer.

The child becomes a little more independent if he can put every object in the correct box: the ball, for example, belongs in a box that has a picture of exactly the same ball stuck on it and stays in the recreation area; the screw belongs in the work corner in a box with a picture of exactly the same sort of screw. It is like doing a puzzle in space (a strength of autistic people). Even if the child does not understand at first that the screw is a symbol for the work period, he still associates the object with a place. You bring a screw to a place where there is an identical screw. That is the place where the activity takes place . . . understanding comes later.

Learning to recognize the events of the day involves considerable individualization:

1. The first stage involves duration. A 'daily timetable' for certain children may mean simply showing them the predictability of two activities, for example first work, then play (that is the usual basis: learning to recognize that there is a certain rhythm in life. Sometimes you do one thing before another, 'work' for example; after that you can do what you like: 'play'). Later a half-day can be announced. After that, perhaps an entire day. Then a work schedule, then a monthly calendar . . . depending on possibilities.

2. The second stage concerns training. At first you physically lead the child from one place to another. Then you give him the object and he takes it himself to the correct place (on the way he holds the object in his hand so he can constantly 'feel' it and not forget what he is planning to do). Later he may only need to look at the object to know at once what is expected of him.

3. The third stage concerns the choice of symbols. The most important thing here is to keep the following thought in mind: it is not the highest or most abstract form of symbol that is important, but the highest form of independence. You can work with objects as described above, pictures (drawings, photos) or the written word. There are also all kinds of form in between: change-over forms, objects stuck on cards, objects with a drawing next to them, pictures with a written text underneath whereby the text gradually becomes larger and the drawing smaller. It is important always to prepare the children thoroughly for a new symbol at their work table (for example by teaching them to put the pictures next to objects or written words next to pictures). Only when they have fully understood the connection in the simplest situation, where only the essential information is present and they are protected from excess, and therefore disturbing, information are they ready to use these new insights in a more complicated context at home and in the classroom, where they are less protected from extraneous and distracting information, such as a baby brother crying, the TV blaring or another pupil walking from the work corner to the recreation area. And, with a risk of repeating myself, we must not always go for what we call the 'highest' level, i.e. the kind of help most useful to us. Acceptance also means accepting differences, accepting that someone is different and needs to be helped in a different way. After all, what do we want for someone who is autistic? That he is happy in his own way or that he resembles us as much as possible?

2.7. The :How long?' question. On work and other schedules

Objects and pictures give a visual answer to the questions 'when' and
'where'. However, if a pupil knows that he is expected at his work
table at a particular moment, he also wants to know how long his
activities there will last. Try explaining that to someone who has no,
or limited, verbal ability, has no understanding of time and no real
understanding of quantity. Again it comes down to presenting
abstract information in a concrete way: the invisible and cursory
becomes visible and durable. We will also teach 'how long' in the
most organized situation (the work table), so that the pupil will also
understand 'duration' in a situation that may not be as well adapted
to his needs.

Our pupil with autism, then, is sitting at the work table. We know
that he will do something meaningful there, but he does not yet know
this. His experiences have perhaps been different. We are busy developing a new routine and work habits. We know that he will later
come to like this, but at the moment he may perhaps be fighting a
new routine, as he often does when faced with new situations. That is
why it is so important for him to understand how long this situation
will continue.

I sometimes wonder what I would do if people put me in a very
difficult situation, asked me to carry out some task that is very hard
for me and gave me no information about how long it would last – I
would have behaviour problems in less confused circumstances. If,
on the other hand, someone told me it would only last 5 to 10
minutes, I would find it easier to accept the difficulties; there would
be an end in sight.

People with autism also want an end in sight. We invite the child
to come to the work table, yes, but for how long? We have a work
schedule for this, a plan that shows all the tasks that have to be
finished. This could be a colour schedule, in which every colour indicates a different task. A red card on the plan indicates the box on the
left with the same red colour, the green card indicates the green box,
the blue card points to the blue box. When there are no more colour
cards to be seen on the plan, the work has ended. (A similar plan
could, of course, work with numbers: 1 symbolizes the first task, 2 the
second, and 3 the third, etc. When all the numbers have disappeared
from the plan, the work session is over. Incidentally, the use of
numbers does not depend on a child's numerical comprehension.
He can learn that 1,2,3 do not indicate a quantity, but a sequence. 1
is what you do first 2 comes after that, 3 is next).

Children who have problems putting colours together or using numbers can learn to work independently at a lower level, with objects. The duration of the work session is then simply shown by the number of work boxes placed to his left on his table: three boxes on the left symbolizes three tasks to be completed. If the three boxes have moved from left to right, the work is over. (Why from left to right and not from right to left? This is mainly culturally determined: in our culture people learn to read and write from left to right, and many other activities are oriented from left to right. It makes sense to preserve this cultural choice, even for left-handed children). Even at this simple level a child experiences clarity and predictability. If there are no more objects on his left and everything has been moved to the right, 'work time' is over. The pupil may have no numerical concepts and little understanding of time, but he can still, understand us. Objects 'talk', left is 'to be done', right is 'done'. Concrete objects have replaced abstract concepts.

2.8. On 'how to do' a task. How is this organized?

Let's begin simply, as this point is always the biggest hurdle. Students keep hearing this during the training sessions. They then go to their own class or living group, and develop activities there that are much easier than the ones done before, yet they are still on too high a level.

Here is an example. We use baskets that always hold one task, in this case a sorting task. The pupils take the basket from the left and put it on the work table. Where? On the left of the work table? In the middle? To the right? It is easiest if they put the basket on the right of the table. Then it is ready when the task is completed, when everything has to be cleared away. To help the child to remember this, we make the place for the basket more visible with coloured sticky tape.

First, it has to be unpacked. There are three boxes in the basket, one containing bolts and Lego blocks (these go on the left), another box with a bolt stuck on it (as a way of showing him that the bolts have to go in there) and one with a Lego block stuck on it (this is where the Lego blocks go). It can't be more simple. Yet this task is still far too difficult for many pupils with autism who can otherwise work independently. They become very confused unpacking the box, they organize the task badly and develop behaviour problems. By giving them more visual clarity we can prevent these behaviour problems. For example, we can mark the table with the numbers 1,2 and 3. If the pupils find the boxes in the basket, they see that they carry the numbers 1,2,3. We teach them to put the 1 on the 1, the 2 on the 2 and the 3 on the 3 (Figure 2.11). All the boxes are now in the right order and the pupils can organize their tasks independently, something initially impossible. A similar system can be worked out using colours: blue on blue, red on red, yellow on yellow.

For pupils who are very bad at organization, we can work out 'one-box' tasks. Everything is preorganized. There are three

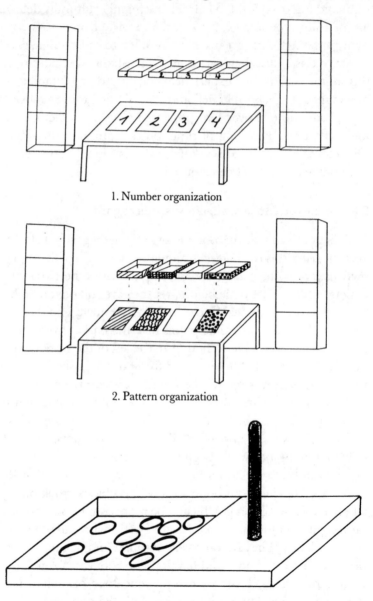

1. Number organization

2. Pattern organization

3. One-box organization

Figure 2.11

compartment in one box. The child takes the entire preorganized task from the left, completes it and puts in on the right. Task finished.

It is not a matter of knowing and following 'recipes' but of understanding the reasoning behind the recipes. The basic idea is this: prepare the children for as independent an adult life as possible. Independence is in itself dependent on the way we adapt the environment and the activities to them. Through these adapted tasks we make them more independent and less dependent on our help: they have better control of the situation and develop a feeling of self-respect. Adapted tasks, then, have a direct and positive emotional effect. By giving children the chance to succeed more often and to fail less, one reduces the need for stereotyped behaviour and also encounters fewer behaviour problems.

Ordinary children feel competent when they play. Children with autism feel competent when they work.

2.9. Concrete rewards as a means of motivation. 'Why' questions

Most of us spend a lot of time earning money. If this motivation were dropped, we would work much less. Now we know that money is not much of a stimulus for most people with autism. If you have difficulty seeing 'behind' things, money is no more than a piece of paper.

We do a lot of things for the status they bring or from other 'higher' motives: for the good of mankind, from solidarity, a feeling of justice, etc. All these 'whys' are at such an impenetrable social level that they mostly fail to inspire someone with autism to work. How then can we make all the activities we offer them 'meaningful' on a level that they can understand. Initially, this will happen through rewards. I know from experience that if someone wants to persuade me to do something difficult, they do well to offer me a very concrete bribe – a bottle of good wine or good food perhaps.

Ordinary children create a lot of energy from social contacts: these are rewarding in themselves. They want to be the way their mother and father would like them to be, they copy their sister or brother. (The story goes that a triathlon athlete was once asked to do as much as a socially active toddler aged 2;6 years. After 4 hours he was exhausted.) This sort of energy is lacking in most children with autism. However, we still want our pupils to experience rewards: their life is much harder than ours so they need the rewards that much more. The only difference is that their tastes are sometimes extraordinary. They may end up wanting rewards that seem very strange to us, such as holding a toy car, swinging a rope, etc.

During the developmental period, food or drink may be the only rewards that motivate them. One then uses these, coupled with lots of 'well done!', 'very good!' etc. in the hope that the praise will become more important and that these rewards can be dropped. In any case the children must learn that you don't get something for nothing. We ask difficult things of them, things that may seem pointless to them at the time, and therefore they should feel rewarded when they do them. I think it is good for them to visualize the reward, perhaps by putting a picture of it at the bottom of their work schedule or on the daily timetable itself. When they enter the classroom or join the living group they can see the symbol of rewards at regular intervals: 'Someone has thought of me, they understand me, they love me.' Happily, experience shows that visual clarity and the feeling of success alone works as rewards. Often the ability to 'see' the final goal, to be able to get an overview of the entire task (beginning and end) is sufficient motivation in itself. A conceptual, social 'why' is replaced here by its perceptual equivalent: seeing the final goal is sometimes enough of a motivation. Strongly individualized work periods then become the time when everything works: during their free time they are often devastated once more by the same old problems, and then things can go wrong again.

2.10. The most common questions in connection with the plans described

1. Should parents use similar schedules at home?

We have set up the adaptation of the environment in a training session in an improvised classroom. Parents can get inspiration from the examples we have given. We know many parents who, with guidance from professionals, have adapted space and timetables at home for their children. Of course one cannot expect parents to arrange their homes like a classroom. The work with parents is also fully individualized and involves listening to their needs and priorities, taking the wishes of the entire family into account.

2. Do such plans encourage cognitive inflexibility? Can one overcondition children with autism?

A slogan-like answer is: if I talk to you and you understand me, do you feel you are being conditioned? Of course not. Our plans are simply a form of communication.

Someone who does not understand speech or has difficulty using it learns to understand a visual language. Just like ordinary language, understanding is the first step. As soon as a pupil knows the system, he will actively try to manage it. We all know children who have their own schedules at home or at school. First they eat, then listen to music, then go to the swimming pool, then to riding school, then to the supermarket, etc.

It is obviously very satisfying for us if we see that children begin to understand the systems, but when they have reached this stage it is necessary for them to learn to differentiate between the sequence of activities and their own preferences. You can teach them where the 'communication cards' for activities are so that they can choose for themselves, but just like ordinary children they also have to learn that certain choices are impossible at certain times.

There is, of course, a danger that they develop a certain rigidity in following the schedules, particularly if the daily timetable always has the same activities in the same sequence. It is important to teach the children how to cope with changes and new experiences. For that reason, once they have understood the symbolic values of daily timetables, for example, we announce new activities via pictures or objects, to change the schedule.

We have discovered that the standard cliché – children with autism cannot cope with changes in their routine – is not true. They do have problems with unannounced changes. That is normal; we experience this ourselves. If we have a certain pattern of expectation in connection with something important to us (a visit to the theatre or cinema) and a minute before we are about to start out we are told the trip is off, we also have trouble accepting it. Then we may exhibit 'behaviour problems'. However, if we are told nicely some 4 hours ahead that the concert is cancelled but we will be going to a good restaurant instead, we feel better about it. We can announce things in a similar way to our pupils with autism: 'I'm so sorry, we can't go to the swimming pool today. But look at the timetable: we're going to listen to some music.' Moreover, we must not forget that all these schedules 'evolve'. Some children may start by working with objects and end up being able to use written instructions.

We have also talked about hanging schedules in a fixed position in the classroom or at home, but for the more gifted pupils with autism more flexible portable systems can be worked out. The sequence of activities can, for example, be written in a notebook. Then, after every activity, the pupil crosses it out – finished. It begins to look like an ordinary child's school timetable.

The schedules should also be tried out in various places: first in the classroom, then at home, and later in other places as well and with other people. And finally, although we have started off talking about daily timetables, these can eventually grow into work schedules – weekly, monthly and even yearly schedules. But once again, how far we go with this depends mainly on the possibilities for independent use of our efforts by the pupil with autism himself.

3. When do you begin to cut back the use of schedules?

To be slightly cynical, when do you take away a blind person's cane and Braille? Taking away the schedules too quickly can result in taking away the person's independence after building it up so carefully. It is indeed a question of balance. Too many visual aids or visual aids beneath the child's level can, of course, have a suffocating effect (aids above his level are even worse). But the danger, at least in professional circles, is more likely to be in cutting them back too soon, thinking he now knows everything by heart. We have seen children with autism cope for some time without visual aids. Then behaviour problems that had disappeared for years crop up again.

From the children's standpoint, this is understandable. They can fall back on their reserves for some time, they can cope with the initial frustrations, but when the clarity and predictability (which are their consolation in a difficult existence) completely disappear, chaos takes over and, with it, the behaviour problems.

So we return to the crucial problem: what do we want for these children? A difficult life that resembles our own as much as possible, or an easier life suited to their own needs? Can you accept the handicap of autism as it is? Professionals often find this more difficult than parents.

Chapter 3
Communication

Certain loud noises such as the school bell ringing hurt my ears like a
dentist drill hitting a nerve and made my heart race.

Grandin, 1992

1. The 'inflexible cognitive style' of people with autism

The difficulty these people face in interpreting and understanding
what they observe is reflected in the main characteristics of autism:
qualitative impairments in the development of communication,
social interaction and imagination. Let us deal first with the problem
of communication, and in particular, echolalia (the literal repetition
of words) as an example of what is meant by 'qualitative impairments' in the definition of autism.

1.1. 'Qualitative impairments': echolalia as an example

Be careful. The characteristics of autism must not be given too
absolute a character. Echolalia (the literal repetition of words or
sentences, immediate or delayed) is often associated with autism.
Indeed, studies have shown that most young verbal people with
autism have echolalic characteristics. However, echolalia is not in
itself an essential feature of autism. In normal language development
all children show forms of echolalia. For a specific period in their
development it is normal to be echolalic.

One also find echolalia among mentally retarded children without autism, but here echolalia is normal for their mental age (for
example, a mental age of 22 months). So, if echolalia is associated

47

only with delay (a quantitative aspect) in development, it is not a symptom of autism. Echolalia can only be considered a characteristic of autism if it is present in spite of a higher mental age. For a child with autism and a mental age of 5, it would not be normal still to be echolalic. There it may be considered as a 'qualitative impairment'.

As you read the following notes on early development, it is important to keep in mind that little is known for certain about the first 2 years in the life of the child with autism. Even less is known about individual variations. And when autism is accompanied by a mental handicap the behaviour described develops even later. So do not respond immediately by saying, 'But my son was not like that at all.' The following tables of development (Table 3.1 and 3.2) are taken from an article by Marcus and Watson. I would recommend reading the entire article for a full interpretation of the table.

After this short overview, we shall now try to place some of the most important characteristics of communication seen in young autistic people within the context of their particular cognitive style. How do we know that these children face specific problems as they acquire communication skills and try to assimilate the meaning of what they see and hear?

1.2. Communication and a rigid cognitive style

A comparative study by Menyuk and Quill (1985) provides exciting information on this subject. They studied the early development of meaning in language with non-handicapped children and with autistic children. (It should be understood, here and in other examples, that we are speaking of children with specific levels of development. The examples should not be used to generalize about all children with autism.) It has been shown that, during the earliest stages of language acquisition, ordinary children typically make mistakes of over-generalization. For example, they understand the connection between a sound, such as 'chair', and the object 'chair'. For a short period, however, they have a tendency also to call a sofa, stool or bench a 'chair'.

Similarly, small children may call an object a 'glass' but also use the same word for a cup or beaker and even a bottle, as they are all objects from which to drink. Afterwards, they realize their mistake and correct themselves. What is interesting about these mistakes is that one can see how their minds work. They have an intuitive tendency to be led by meaning rather than by perception as they develop knowledge. The most important thing in their understanding of the word 'chair' is not the actual visible appearance of a chair, but the meaning behind it: that it is something to sit on.

Table 3.1. Aspects of normal development during preschool years: language and communication

Age in months

2   Cooing, vocal-type sounds
6   Vocal 'conversations' or turn-taking in face-to-face
    Position with parent
    Consonant sounds emerging
8   Varies intonation in babbling, including questioning
    Intonation
    Repetitive syllable babbling (ba-ba-ba, ma-ma-ma)
    Pointing gesture emerging
12 First words emerging
    Use of jargon with sentence-like intonation
    Language most frequently used for commenting on environment and vocal play
    Uses gestures plus vocalization to get attention, show objects and make requests
18 3–50 word vocabulary
    Beginning to put two words together
    Over extension of word meanings (e.g. 'daddy' refers to all men)
    Uses language to comment, request objects and actions, and get attention
    Also pulls people to get and direct attention
    May 'echo' or imitate frequently
24 3–5 words combined at times ('telegraphic' speech)
    Asks simple questions (e.g. Where Daddy? Go bye-bye?)
    Uses 'this' accompanied by pointing gestures
    Calls self by name rather than 'I'
    May briefly reverse pronouns
    Cannot sustain topic of conversation
    Language focuses on here and now
36 Vocabulary of about 1000 words
    Most grammatical morphemes (plural, past tense, prepositions, etc.)
    used appropriately
    Echoing infrequent by this age
    Language increasingly used to talk about 'there' and 'then'
    Much questioning, often more to continue interaction than to seek
    information
48 Complex sentence structures used
    Able to sustain topic of conversation and add new information
    Will ask others to clarify utterances
    Adjusts quality of language depending on listener (e.g. simplifies language to a 2-
    year-old)
60 More appropriate use of complex structures
    General mature grammatical structure (still some problems with
    subject/verb agreement, irregular forms, pronoun case, etc.)
    Ability to judge sentences as grammatical/ungrammatical and make
    corrections
    Developing understanding of jokes and sarcasm, recognition of verbal
    ambiguities
    Increasing ability to adjust language according to listener's perspective and
    role

Table 3.2. Early development in autism: language and communication

---

Age in months

---

6   Crying is difficult to interpret
8   Limited or unusual babbling (e.g. squeals or screeches)
    No imitation of sounds, gestures, expressions
12 First words may appear, but often not used meaningfully
    Frequent, loud crying; remains difficult to interpret
24 Usually fewer than 15 words
    Words appear, then drop out
    Gestures do not develop; few point to objects
36 Word combinations rare
    May echo phrases, but no creative language use
    Odd rhythm, tone or stress
    Poor articulation in about half of speaking children
    Half or more are without meaningful speech
    Takes parent by hand and leads to object
    Goes to customary location and waits to be given object
48 A few combine two or three words creatively
    Echolalia persists; may be used communicatively
    Mimics TV commercials
    Makes requests

(From Watson, L. and Marcus, L., Diagnosis and assessment of preschool children. In Schopler, E. and Mesibov, G. (eds) *Diagnosis and assessment in autism*. London, Plenum Press, 1988.)

In the earliest phases of language development in children with autism, one does not find this kind of mistake – in fact, the opposite is often true. A child with autism will have a tendency to use the sound 'chair' for one particular chair, of a particular height, a particular colour, on four legs. From his point of view, it does not make sense that objects that are bigger, a different colour or with three legs would be given the same name. His basic understanding, based on what he sees, is too limited to make spontaneous generalizations possible. (It is important to be aware that this is not in itself a hopeless statement. I do not mean that young people with autism cannot generalize at all, only that one should be conscious that they may not have the ability to make spontaneous generalizations possible. If they do not, they will need outside help.)

What I noticed about Thomas's early language development was that he made up his own names for different objects which were really the same, but didn't look exactly alike. For various things we call 'bicycle' he had other names. He had a 'bicycle', a 'tractor', a 'wheels in the mud', a 'wheels in the grass' and also a 'feet on the pedals'. Everyone called him a 'creative young man', but I knew that it had more to do with helplessness. He didn't understand what I meant when I said 'get on your bicycle' if his 'feet on the pedals' was in front of him. He couldn't understand that we called his 'feet on the pedals' a bicycle as well.

Hilde De Clercq

1.3. What is 'big'? What is 'small'? The case of a big mouse and a small elephant

We have been talking about the acquisition of the simplest words: words for things that you can see, hear, taste: words which belong to specific categories.

'Relational words' – such as 'big', 'small', 'wide', 'narrow', 'on', 'over', 'afterwards', 'give' and 'take' – are more difficult to acquire because they take their meaning from their surroundings, their relationship to other words in a sentence and/or the external context.

> If Thomas sees that his father has brought me flowers, he always shouts, 'Let me take them!' He really means 'give'. Later he says, 'Now they are mother's flowers because I took them.' The meaning of give and take is difficult for him. The other day he saw a vase of flowers on the table. He insisted that the flowers weren't mine but his; you see he hadn't given them to me yet.

Hilde De Clercq

'Big' and 'small' are easy concepts for us, but they cause real problems for a child with autism. Teachers often say, 'I have tried to show him in every way possible and he still doesn't understand. Why not?' To understand, we must enter his mind and look at the world from his point of view. To enable him to understand the concept of big and small, we would have to be able to explain it in terms of an absolute definition and, unfortunately, this is impossible. Look at Figure 3.1. Is this glass big or small?

In the first context, the glass is small in comparison to the bottle, but in the second context, it is big compared with the spoon. To use simple words such as 'big' and 'small', one must first put them into context. This demands a mental flexibility that young people with autism may not have. Statements such as 'This is a big mouse' and 'This is a small elephant' are virtually incomprehensible if you hold to absolute meanings and have difficulty understanding 'big' and 'small' in their relative senses. A word such as 'in' is easy to understand if you are 'in' the house, but what if you'll be back 'in' 2 weeks? Where is the base for observation; where is the predictability if first you can see 'in' (in the house) and later you can't.

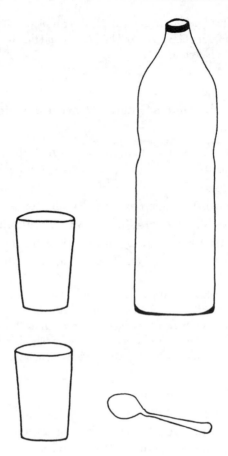

Figure 3.1 Is this glass big or small?

1.4. When do you say 'you'? When do you say 'I'?

Similar problems with mental flexibility are found in the switch of personal pronouns: the jump from 'I' to 'you'. Many young people with autism have difficulties using 'I' and 'you' correctly. In early psychoanalytical literature, this was seen as proof that people with autism consciously refused to develop an identity of their own; the way they systematically did not use 'I' was seen as symbolic of this. However, purely from observation, it is not obvious that a person is sometimes called 'I', sometimes 'you', or 'he' ('He did it'), or 'we' or 'they' (in groups). This demands a mental flexibility that many people with autism lack. It does not have to do with a reluctance to use the 'I'. If you ask a child with autism, 'Do you want a biscuit?' when he is learning language, he will repeat 'Do you want a biscuit?' when he means 'I'. 'John wants a biscuit' or 'I want a biscuit' will also be repeated as easily as 'Do you want a biscuit?'

The next example serves to illustrate movingly the literal way in which people with autism think and how this can lead to misunderstandings with professionals who do not understand such a literal turn of mind. Take note of the enormous efforts Tom makes to talk like us.

> Tom is a 10-year-old high-functioning autistic child in a normal class. The teacher cannot understand why someone like him, who can learn things by heart so easily, can be called 'autistic'. Tom is guided by a very capable speech therapist. One day Tom asks him the highly intelligent question, 'Who is 'I'?' Quite a poser . . . Luckily the speech therapist understands the need for visual support for people with autism, particularly when it comes down to abstract understandings. He hits his chest with his hand and says, 'Look, Tom. Everyone who can thump his chest like this can call himself 'I'.' Tom immediately tries it himself. He finds it funny: Tom is 'I'. During the first period of this new learning process, you see him bravely hitting himself on his chest every time, for example, that he says, 'Tom, I'm going home' (his Christian name has to be there for safety). In the second phase he becomes bolder; he leaves 'Tom' out. 'I'm going home.' During this period he looks intensely at the others: is it all right to hit his chest when he hears 'I'? In the third phase he gets even more courageous. He now just says, 'I'm going home' while holding his hands tightly behind his back. For him that must be like stepping into the void. Around this time the speech therapist meets Tom's teacher, who says, 'I don't know if Tom's autistic or not, but I think he has a much bigger problem. It seems to me that he's sexually overdeveloped, even a bit perverse.'
> 'What's happened?'
> 'I don't know what's got into him, but recently he has been staring at my breasts.'
> The speech therapist immediately realized what was wrong and asked,
> 'Does he perhaps look at your breasts when you say the word 'I'?
> And that was it.

1.5. Echolalia as an attempt to belong

If we understand the problems that children with autism have learning simple words, we can also imagine why so many of their sentences have an echolalic character and why their use of language often lacks creativity and inventiveness, limiting itself to the literal repetition of sentences which someone else has said.

Anecdotes often speak more than pages of theory, so first some examples.

Liz is 5 years old. She doesn't speak but she can sing around five songs by heart. She sings the words 'water, 'milk', 'bread', but if she's hungry or thirsty, she just takes her mother's hand and leads her to the kitchen. Why won't she say that she wants some milk? After all, she knows the word. Sometimes people say, 'I told you so. She can do it, but she won't.' But there is a big difference between a word repeated and a word used creatively. When singing songs by heart we are using processes in the right side of the brain. A word and a melody are not analysed for meaning, but are stored in the brain in a rather superficial way and repeated later. To use a word creatively you must first analyse its meaning, and that process takes place in the left side of the brain. Liz has not yet reached the stage of analysing for meaning. That will come later. Now she can't do it.

Brian says, 'Close the door' when he wants to be left alone. It is easy to understand why. When his mother takes him to his room at difficult moments, so he can calm down she always says, 'I'll close the door', and then she goes away and Brian is left alone. Brian also says, 'Well done' if he doesn't like some chore he has to do, such as the washing up. For Brian, 'Well done' has gradually come to mean the chore is finished. Now, 'Well done' also means 'I don't feel like starting it.'

In the literature on autism the 'permanence of the original learning situation' is often referred to. It means that expressions like Brian's have a very concrete origin and continue to retain the same meaning. You can come across this again and again. Here for example, it is simple: Brian is in an autism class where teachers encourage him all day, both for the efforts he makes and the completion of a job.

A clearer understanding of delayed echolalia contradicts the cliché of the autistic child who avoids contact. One finds that the opposite is true, that those with autism do attempt to take part in conversation, they do attempt to communicate, they simply do it with the limited means at their disposal. For example, when Jeremy wants to listen to music he always says, 'Hands off the radio, you'll break it.' This is because he hears this sentence every time he goes near the radio. He wants to explain, 'I want to listen to the music'. But those around don't understand this. In fact echolalia is not so unusual. If a child who is not handicapped is asked to do something in a language he understands, he will carry it out. If you say, 'Get the book', he will get the book. If you use other words beyond his understanding, he will have a tendency to repeat them verbatim. If you say 'Abracadabra book', he may repeat 'Abracadabra book'.

Moreover, an echolalic style is not uncommon in early language development. Research into normal language development refers to 'word babies' and 'intonation babies'. Word babies use normal means of learning language. Their first words are really one word sentences: 'milk' means 'I want a drink of milk, give me some milk.' The meaning is derived from the word. Intonation babies are much more interested in the social side of things. They reproduce a series

of words without bothering about the meaning. It is like a game. I
normal development children can choose either strategy. Children
with autism do not have this choice. They cannot do it any other
way. We ourselves might use echolalic intonation strategies if we
wanted to communicate in a language we have not studied. Imagine
that you are in Spain and you do not know any Spanish. You hear a
long series of word – tengohambrequierocomer – but you cannot
pick out individual words. You don't know that ' *tengo*' means 'I have',
'*hambre*' means 'hunger', '*quiero*', 'I want', and '*comer*', to eat. Thus
you are likely to repeat the whole sentence instead of the suitable
word.

Some expressions of delayed echolalia may seem bizarre but they
become more comprehensible when the background is understood.
Many echolalic expressions are full of attempts to communicate. The
following quotation illustrates this:

> I was once asked by somebody why I repeat the same phrase exactly as I
> had heard it and in a similar voice to the person who said it. I had no
> answer at the time. Being asked to write this paper I have had to think more
> deeply about myself than I have ever had to before. I now know that there
> are several answers. First, you have to work so hard in order to understand
> speech, that when the words do eventually go into your brain they seem to
> become imprinted in the way you hear them. Second, because trying to
> speak is quite an effort, particularly when you are just starting to learn to
> speak, it is all you can do to just try and reproduce what your good memory
> knows. Third, for a long time you have so little idea about speech and it is
> all such an effort that you seem to believe that the voice of the person used
> to say the words is the way you, too, have to say them. You do not seem to
> be aware that the words can be put across using all different kinds of voices
> and that there are alternative ways of expressing things. It was only from
> my academic work that I picked up the fact that there is more than one
> correct way of saying things. Fourth, sometimes I used to repeat the same
> words over again as this made me feel safer. Fifth, when I first started
> repeating back phrases exactly as I had heard them, I think I did this as I
> was only able to come out with one or two words for myself so it seemed to
> be a good way of experimenting with longer sentences even if they weren't
> thought out by me.

Therese Joliffe et al., 1992

1.6. The origin of an echolalic formula is often unknown

The meaning of an echolalic utterance is often not easy to discover. I
still don't understand where Eric picked up 'the trains are leaving'
but it is his way of saying 'now it's getting too difficult for me.' It is his
way of warning us: if you don't do something, the cat will be among

the pigeons. Eric's parents do not know the origin of this expression either. One can only assume that he was once in a difficult situation which he wanted to leave, and at that moment heard someone say 'The trains are leaving' and coincidentally he was also allowed to go. He now thinks this is the right way to ask. The original learning situation has acquired a permanent character. Eric asks in the way he is able to ask instead of the way he should. If you ignore him for a minute or two after he says, 'The trains are leaving', he has a behavioural crisis – but you were warned!

Leo Kanner wrote about a boy who is just about to drop his dog off the balcony. Mother realizes that rapid intervention is essential. With a very expressive face she calls out, 'Don't throw the dog off the balcony!' Bewildered, he puts the dog down. He may not understand why his mother is so upset – the meaning may have escaped him – but the warning clearly has an effect. A few days later the same boy is sitting by himself and he is having great fun. He has just discovered some containers that all have wonderful white substances inside. He has thrown the sugar all over the floor, then the salt, the flour, and now the rice. It's a feast for the eye. But then mother arrives with the same expression on her face as the other day. Before she can say anything the boy exclaims, 'Don't throw the dog off the balcony!'

Thus echolalia (here, delayed echolalia) is usually not a meaningless use of language as was once thought ('Stop repeating') but rather an attempt to take control of a situation with the limited means available. When it is impossible to do this within the left hemisphere – where you analyse what you see for meaning – you then change over to the right hemisphere where you take what you see as it is, without translation.

About half the people with autism are verbal. Seventy-five per cent of them make clear echolalic utterances, while for the other 25 per cent, the utterances are less clear. With slight exaggeration one can say that normal people have the ability to get through the day by constantly using new word combinations, which we adapt to changing circumstances and the status and interests of our fellow conversationalists. That sort of flexibility is too difficult for even the most gifted autistic people. Much more often than we do, they fall back on expressions and sentences they have learned by heart from others.

1.7. The difficult metaphor: taking the figurative literally

Other problems which autistic people with verbal ability face are caused by figurative expressions, abstract words that are too 'elusive' and words with double meanings. The examples are legion:

- When a boy was told after a walk in the rain that he had to wipe his feet, he took off his shoes and socks and wiped his feet on the mat.
- A boy panicked when he heard his mother say she wanted to cry her eyes out.
- When a mother said the sugar had run out, her son began to look for a hole.
- Father and uncle were talking about a lucky friend. 'He hit the jackpot', they said. 'That must have hurt', said the autistic son.
- A boy insisted on putting his bicycle inside every evening. The parents only understood why several weeks later: their son had heard someone say, 'Night is falling.'
- An autistic boy heard someone talking about his uncle who was ill. 'He's been nailed to his bed for three weeks'. The boy ran to tell his mother, 'Uncle John is nailed to his bed', he says, 'and he's so nice.'

1.8. Language as an expression of fragmentary thinking

If the 'normal' meaning of words is changed, autistic children can become very confused.

Brian runs downstairs looking for his mother, crying 'pipi, pipi, pipi.' She realizes that there is a problem and goes to see what it is. Brian has been playing with his brother Peter. Mother goes upstairs to take a look. Peter has made a tent by hanging a sheet over a table and has asked his autistic brother, 'Come and play in the house.' The sight of the sheet and the table has shocked Brian: a sheet over a table is not his idea of a house. Such figurative use of words causes him to panic. The world is difficult enough without trying to reinvent it.

The following story would be a real horror story for people with autism. The story was actually written by Eugene Ionesco for 'ordinary' children. Every morning little Josette creeps into bed with her father and asks him to tell her a story. One morning he decides to explain the 'real' meaning of words:

> Josette says to her papa: 'Are you talking on the telephone?'
> Papa hangs up. He says, 'This is not a telephone'.
> 'Yes, it is,' Josette answers. 'Mama told me so. Jacqueline said so too'.
> 'Your Mama and Jacqueline are wrong,' Papa says. 'Your Mama and Jacqueline don't know what it's called. It's called a cheese'.
> 'That's called a cheese?', asks Josette. 'Then people are going to think it's made of cheese'.
> 'No.' says Papa, 'because cheese isn't called cheese. It's called music box. And the music box is a rug. The rug is called lamp. The ceiling is

called floor. The floor is called ceiling. The wall is called a door'.

So Papa teaches Josette the real meaning of words. A chair is a window. The window is a penholder. A pillow is a piece of bread. Bread is a bedside rug. Feet are ears. Arms are feet. A head is a behind. A behind is a head. Eyes are fingers. Fingers are eyes.

Then Josette speaks the way her father teaches her. She says: 'I look out the chair while eating my pillow. I walk with my ears. I have ten eyes to walk with and two fingers to look with. I sit down with my head on the floor. I put my behind on the ceiling. When I have eaten my music box, I put jam on the bedside rug, for a good dessert. Take the window, Papa, and draw me some pictures'.

And the end of the story goes like this:

Suddenly Mama arrives, like a flower, in her flowered dress, carrying flowers, with her flowered pocketbook, her flowered hat, her eyes like flowers, her mouth like a flower.

'What have you been doing out so early?' Papa asks.

'Gathering flowers', Mama says.

And Josette says: 'Mama, you opened that wall'.

Ordinary children love to turn the world upside down, but for children with autism, it is terrifying. It is already difficult enough to understand the world in its literal sense. If everything can mean the opposite as well, then no thank you. The most gifted people with autism, who have large vocabularies, who do not seem to have many difficulties with syntax or word sequence, still have problems differentiating between major and minor issues.

I was born on March 19th in Ghent, in the Bijloke hospital. My mother, Marguerite R., gave me milk from her breast and I started to drink. Years later when Maarten was three, he started to go to the Gaspard de Coligny school which was built in 1934. I went to the nursery school. Later Miss V.K. and Miss B. discovered that Maarten was impossible at this school and my mother and father Boud ewijn J. thought to themselves 'The boy will never get better.' Then my mother thought about taking me to a doctor in Antwerp and at that moment they discovered that I was seriously handicapped and autistic at the same time. They didn't know what would happen to me (1968).

From 1964 we lived in the Patijntjes street in Ghent. My mother heard from another women who was very wise that it would be best for him to go to the Netherlands. To take speaking lessons.

In Reek we had Miss C. and Miss Biney say that I couldn't do anything. My parents prayed a lot for me that I would sometime learn to speak and from 1971 I could say a couple of sentences. In Reek Children's Home I unconsciously stayed outside the group of other boys because I was afraid of what they would do to me, who unconsciously behaved abnormally. Then I began to be interested in wheels, rode on the go-cart and cycled in the play-ground.

I began to kick the ball and fell on the hard ground of stone. My knee began to bleed. Through my bad behaviour unconsciously I broke a window with the feet and J. the assistant gave me a hard box on the ears and I had to stand in a corner.

Maarten Jonckheere

The social rules of conversation are another stumbling block. When do you start a conversation? How long can you talk about what interests you? When should you ask someone if he's still inter-ested? George, who has written a book on meteorology, can talk about it impressively, but when he asks you for the twentieth time if you know how the weather changed during the afternoon of July 22nd 1949, it can be too much of a good thing. A dialogue with high-functioning individuals with autism often risks becoming a mono-logue since putting yourself in someone else's position demands too much mental flexibility. They have words enough; it is ideas that are difficult. Their world is different. Or ours is. Ours is so difficult to understand. Now and then they ask questions, they say things which are painful reminders that they are more handicapped than we sometimes think.

On a visit to the Antwerp zoo, one such gifted autistic boy asked, 'The dart that you shoot to drug the snake, how deep does it go into the body?' He found it incomprehensible that the guide didn't know the answer down to the millimetre. Why was he a guide if he didn't even know how deep the arrow went? A little later he asked the guide, 'Do snakes slide over a condom when they're having sex?'

Another boy discovered a crack in the classroom wall. 'How long will it take before the crack is four centimetres wide? When will it be thirty centimetres? When will we have to move to the first floor? When will the whole building collapse?'

I became aware that people used language to communicate with one another, but I didn't know how this was done. I got the idea that big words were a sign of intelligence. So to make myself smarter, I decided to read the *Random House Dictionary*. It was the biggest one we had.

That day, after school, I started reading with the first definition. Every day I read as much as I could, concentrating as hard as possible. Nearly eight weeks later I finished the dictionary. I felt a sense of power, and I was eager to have people hear me use these words! I didn't know how to use them in context, I realized a year later. But when I was fifteen I thought I could just substitute a big word for a small one and everyone would say, 'Boy, is he smart!'

When my plan failed I was baffled and hurt. At first I was angry with everyone, but then I knew what it really meant: I still didn't have a clue as to how people talked to one another. Not for the first time, I felt like an alien from outer space – I had no more idea how to communicate with people than a creature from another plant.

Sean Barron, 1992

'Sean, that's just not the way kids talk!' I'd say after hearing him hold forth with a baffled neighbour boy. 'Listen to them – they don't use those kinds of words. You don't have to prove anything to other kids, just be natural! Don't try to impress them with big words, it makes them think you're show-ing off.'

I introduced him to a friend we ran into in a parking lot. Sean said to him, 'My what pleasant nocturnal air we are encountering this evening. It puts me in a very ebullient mood. I'm gratified to meet you.' My friend looked from Sean to me with a smile. Then he laughed, hoping it was safe to do so. I wanted to explain that my fifteen-year-old son had learned English in the Kweichow Province of China.

Sean's Mother

1.9. On forms of communication

Up to now we have been talking about the 50 per cent of people with autism who have reached a reasonable or good verbal level, but what about the others? They nearly all have a lower IQ and a lower level of development. This makes it even more difficult to see the connec-tion between abstract language sounds and the objects, people and happenings for which they stand for.

As verbal communication is too abstract, we must help them by using visual communication systems, in which the connection between symbol and meaning becomes much more visual (iconic). At the same time we must refrain from using sign language as an alternative means of communication for people with autism. Too many of the signs have meanings that are nearly as abstract as words: there are not enough visual connections between the sign and its meaning. That is why the teaching of sign language places too high a cognitive demand on autistic people. They are not as creative as we are; they cannot recreate these signs as easily even if they do under-stand them.

Moreover, abstract signs offer fewer chances of providing the means to integrate into society. Just imagine: an adult with autism who has learned American sign language (Gary Mesibov, director of the TEACCH state program in North Carolina, told me this exam-ple) enters a hamburger restaurant. He stands right in front of the waitress, claps his hands together, turns around, and claps again (the sign for hamburger). The waitress thinks he is mad. What can he be doing? What does he want? Another autistic adult comes in. He communicates with drawings, photos or written language. The waitress thinks, 'I understand. Here's someone who has a communication handicap, he can't talk.' Of course, she wants to help. Communication systems with pictures and photos not only improve the chances of communication because they are more easily understood by everyone, but also make lower cognitive demands. They are more concrete, less arbitrary; there is an immediately recognizable link between an object and its depiction in a drawing. Moreover, the picture does not have to be reinvented each time; it is at hand.

The process of 'reciprocity' in such a communication system with pictures is also made easier as it can be more easily visualized: I ask for something using a picture, I wait, the other gives me what is shown in the picture.

> It was ages before I realized that people speaking might be demanding my attention. But I sometimes got annoyed once I realized that I was expected to attend to what other people were saying because my quietness was being disturbed. I began to start to understand more than just a single word at a time when I realised that speech was sometimes directed at me. At the same time I started reading in my head and writing sentences at school. It was then I found that spoken languages started to frustrate me. I was able to understand words better when they were on paper than when they were said out loud.
>
> *Therese Joliffe et al., 1992*

1.10. Discovering the use of communication

There are, of course, people with autism who have such a low level of development that even a picture is too abstract: they cannot see the connection between something flat and two-dimensional, like a card, and something three-dimensional, like the object itself.

In this case one starts to work first with objects. An ordinary baby with a developmental level of 12 months can already understand the link between an object and an action. If mother shows him the car keys, he knows he is going out. If he sees a plate, it's time to eat. One also starts out with objects for children with autism of a low developmental age. Even if one cannot communicate much with objects, one can still radically influence the childrens' lives if they realize that through the power of communication they can affect their environment. In the end it is the realization that asking for an object is more effective than throwing a tantrum or hurting themselves. The dramatic reality of people with autism is that they often want desperately to communicate but do not know how.

If a child with autism throws himself on the ground or bangs his head against a wall, it is often because he wants to change something in his environment. Unfortunately, his attempt at communication is so vague that we do not understand it. Often such attempts at communication are not directed at anyone in particular: they are not attempts to be sociable. The child finds, however, that indicating a plate, for example, produces more interesting results than throwing a tantrum.

To continue to place the emphasis on speech, to my mind shows an unrealistic understanding of autism. We shouldn't really continue to talk of 'higher' and 'lower' forms of communication. If one is dealing with someone in desperate need of communication, it is the message and not the manner which counts. Take a boy with autism whose tests show he had a developmental age of 14 months but falls below this in communication and social understanding. It is unrealistic to expect such a person to start talking soon. When confronted with such a profile one has no choice: one must start working on a system of communication that falls within his immediate grasp. We can decide later which system of communication he will eventually use. People must not think one has given up all hope of speech if one begins with an alternative communication system. Experience shows the contrary: the more work done on learning to communicate in general, the stronger will be the foundations on which to build later. Finally, those with autism must learn the purpose of communication and the treasures it can bring.

1.11. Seeing is saying (sometimes). Pictures are words made visible

Before we go more deeply into the functions of communication, I want to make a few comments of the use of visual aids for verbal children with autism.

By way of introduction, children go through a phase during normal development in which they talk out loud while playing. Their language steers the game and in a way drives their actions, helping them to organize their activities. After this language becomes internalized and this internal language helps them to perform tasks. There are reasons to believe that for people with autism this is much less the case.

Brian, for example, is a boy who talks but still finds pictures very helpful, both to communicate and to organize his behaviour. He spontaneously uses two-word sentences ('to school', 'eat sandwiches'). Sometimes he seems to talk to himself and to recite series of words like 'bird in a tree', 'duck in the water', 'puss', 'banana'. To outsiders this seems like a pointless exercise, but his parents know that in fact he's leafing through a book in his head. It is a book they have often read to him, with a photo of a duck in the water, a bird in a tree. Brian's verbal language is being developed, but visual communication sometimes helps him more than words to get him over his difficulties. Here are some concrete examples:

1. Brian asks for fruit juice. His mother pours him a glass of apple juice. Brian is not happy. His mother wonders if he wants orange juice and so pours him a second glass. Brian becomes nervous. His mother gives him a glass of pineapple juice. He grows more agitated.

Now mother is also nervous. As always when she doesn't understand him, she points her finger to say, 'show me what you want'. Brian take her to the fridge and shows her he wants an ice lolly. When she sees the box of ice lollies, she understands the problem. The design on the box looks very similar to the design on the bottle of fruit juice. For Brian the visual is more dominant than the verbal.

Brian would find it much easier to indicate the right image with the help of a picture book: 'Here's what I want.' Misunderstandings can be avoided with visual support.

2. The older Brian gets, the more preferences he develops. He knows more and more clearly what he wants and what he doesn't want. His mother has taught him to choose. Before, she would ask, 'Do you want to go swimming or for a walk?' Brian would answer, 'Go for a walk,' But on the way he would have a tantrum. He really wanted to go swimming, but typically if someone asks him a question he would repeat the last word he heard. Now his mother shows him a picture of a swimming pool and a picture of a footpath to represent a walk. Do you want to go swimming or for a walk? Brian understands much better with photos of a pool and a footpath. Oral communication is hard for him, so even though he understands words, pictures speak more clearly.

3. Brian has learned to speak and that is positive, but his interest in spoken language has given rise to new difficulties. Language is so

confusing to him that he sometimes puts his hand over his ears. He seems to want to shut himself off from all the words that interest him but are so hard to understand.

His father has told him that they are going to drive to his grand-parents. Brian enjoys going there. They have a big trampoline. When Brian comes for the weekend the children next door are happy to have a chance to jump on it with him. Brian doesn't speak very well but he can jump. And who else has such a big trampoline at home. They're really lucky to play with Brian.

Brian settles down contentedly in the car. His mother and father and brother Peter begin to talk, mother about going to the beach again, father about work, his brother about school. What's going on? Are we going to the beach, to the office, to school or to grand-mother's? Brian grows restless listening to all the words he can't grasp.

Since then every time they go out in the car they hang up a photo for Brian in the car and say, 'We're going to Granny's' and show him the photo of Granny. Then everything is clearer. Let them talk!

1.12. Functions of communication. Communication IS what communication DOES

Every child, every adolescent, every adult with autism should and must have an individualized communication system: language, pictures, objects . . . A form of communication, adapted to the indi-vidual is the first condition, but this does not guarantee real commu-nication. We have seen examples of this in the descriptions of echolalia – some people use words without realizing the use they serve. Frustration can also arise if the child shows a card without looking at the picture. The pupil with autism may show a card with a picture of scissors when in fact he wants a drink. To communicate truly one has to know the purpose of communication. For some, this must be learned.

> Assumptions that I know things which in fact I don't understand often lead directly to conclusions that I can't learn things which in fact I already know. Such assumptions nearly led to my being placed in an institution. Because I didn't use speech to communicate until I was 12, there was considerable doubt about whether I would ever be able to learn to function indepen-dently. No one guessed how much I understood, because I couldn't say what I knew. And no one guessed the critical thing I didn't know, the one missing connection that so much else depended on: I didn't communicate by talking, not because I was incapable of learning to use language, but because I simply didn't know that was what talking was for. Learning how to talk follows knowing why to talk – and until I learned that words have

meanings, there was no reason to go to the trouble of learning to pronounce them as sounds. Speech therapy was just a lot of meaningless drills in repeating meaningless sounds for incomprehensible reasons. I had no idea that this could be a way to exchange meaning with other minds.

Jim Sinclair, 1992

Communication IS what communication DOES. Does anyone with autism understand the real POWER of communication? That a picture, an object, is a means of influencing your environment? That you are less dependent than you think if you can communicate effectively? That showing a picture of a beaker is more effective than throwing a tantrum when you want a drink? It is a very important and possible goal to teach children with autism that a word, picture or object is a means of influencing the environment, but much harder to teach that these tools can also be a means of changing people's thoughts and feelings.

To learn the purpose of communication is to learn the power of communication. Those who analyse the functions of communication in people with autism get a completely different view, a better one of their real problems, with not only communication, but also their problems in general.

Take the example of Steven, a 26-year-old adult who took part in one of our practical training courses. During practical training sessions on Wednesdays we spend the whole day working on communication. Among other things we observe the functions of communication during the working period, the free-time period and snack time. It is the snack time in particular which often leads to surprising insights. The entire eating situation is consciously 'sabotaged' by us. It is, shall we say, 'environmentally engineered'. In practice this means the following: five young people with autism with varying degrees of verbal and non-verbal skills sit at the table. The teacher in charge begins openly to eat and drink but gives nothing to the children. The agreement is to give food and drink only to those who ask for it (using words, gestures, plates or beakers . . . we're not sadists, by the way: the trainees are told that the pupils will be given their usual meal afterwards).

Steven is the pupil with the largest vocabulary. At the table you can ask him, 'What is this?' and he can answer, 'coke' or 'chocolate'. However, while he has an active vocabulary of at least 1500 works, he uses them for the wrong functions. During the meal you see non-verbal children hold out their beakers (sometimes by copying others), while Steven turns red from anger and frustration. He knows the names of things but he does not know how to use them. He is good at naming (comments about the surroundings: banana, coke . . .), but the ability to ask for objects which he would like to have is underdeveloped.

Does the picture now begin to form? Steven has had traditional 'speech therapy' all his life. What is this? What is that? He has learned to name objects and pictures. The emphasis lies on the 'academic' functions which, while important to our lives, are less so in the lives of someone with severe communication difficulties. To be able to ask for something when you are hungry is, from his point of view, much more important than to be able to name things.

Communication must be taught from the standpoint of the actual need. This conclusion reminds me of the joke about a 5-year-old boy who had never spoken. One day he was sitting at the breakfast table and said, 'The marmalade isn't on the table today.' His parents are stunned. 'You can talk! Proper sentences, even! Why haven't you done this before?' The boy answered, 'Because till now everything was perfect'. Indeed, perhaps the service had been too good.

People try their best to adapt to the needs of those with autism; they try so hard to avoid behavioural problems that they anticipate all the needs of a child with autism before they are expressed. Before you know it, they no longer expect any communication at all. And then eventually there is no more communication. That is why during training programmes, in autism classes and in autism group homes, situations are often 'sabotaged': a need to communicate is created. (This is not done, however, in an attempt to frustrate anyone. In these situations an extra adult is on hand to show how it should be done and to help communicate.)

Not understanding the power of communication is a serious problem of autism. Non-handicapped newborn babies have two different kinds of cry from a very early age. Sometimes they cry because they are hungry, sometimes it is because they want attention. Most mothers recognize the need and its type of cry. Thus normal children develop the ability to ask for something and demand attention in a non-verbal way from a very early age. At the age of around 6 months babies will look their parents in the eye, demand attention or direct their parents' eyes to an object near them which they find interesting, as if to say 'That's pretty!' They have already learned to comment non-verbally.

So it is not simply a question of words: children with autism often do not understand what communication is for:

At this time I had no ability to express my feelings with words. The thought never crossed my mind that I could ask Mom why I was so strange, that I could tell her I needed help. I had no idea that words could be used in this way. Language to me was simply an extension of my compulsions, a tool to use for my own repetitious behaviour.

Sean Barron, 1992

The most important communication functions are (Watson *et al.*, 1989):

1. *Asking for something.* This function can be expressed verbally or non-verbally. 'Banana, please', a picture of a banana, a miniature banana . . . One does not need words only.
2. *Demanding attention.* 'Will you listen to me?', a tap on the shoulder, a ring on a table bell.
3. *Refusing.* 'No', a card with 'too difficult' written on it, an object pushed away . . . Sometimes this function is overdeveloped and can be a problem for teachers. If the function is underdeveloped, it's an even bigger problem for people with autism. Stimulate!

People with autism can learn the three functions above more easily than the following functions. Even so, they may have problems knowing when and how to use these functions.

4. *Making comments* (about visible aspects of the immediate environment). 'An aeroplane!', pointing at a picture on the work table, to the ball, the free-time symbol . . .
5. *Giving information* (about things not immediately visible, the past, the future – this is a more abstract concept). 'What are you going to do tomorrow?' The pupil points to the picture of the swimming pool.
6. *Asking for information.* 'When can I go home?' The pupil points to a picture of a car (symbol for going home).
7. *Communicating emotion.* 'Ouch!' (it hurts). The pupil points to a wound, communicating emotion, but not simply expressing emotion in itself. Children with autism have many emotions, even extreme emotions. If they lie in a corner crying or injure themselves, they may show emotions, but that it not the same as communicating them to someone else. In these cases it is better to refer to 'pre-communicative behaviour': the child perhaps wants to communicate, but does not know how. He needs help but he has not got the right resources at his disposal. We must try to change his pre-communicative behaviour into real communication.

I have suffered a great deal of stomach pain, which started from a very young age which I was unable to tell anybody. It occurs at anytime, but always when I know I have to go somewhere or do something which I know I will find very stressful. Sometimes the pain is so bad that my whole body becomes still and then I am unable to move.

Therese Joliffe et al., 1992

Professionals who have assessed these communication functions have come to the conclusion that non-verbal persons with autism often communicate more than was thought, and also that many people with autism who are verbal communicate less than was generally accepted.

Another result of the study of communication functions is that many professionals have made sense of behaviour that previously seemed pointless. My favourite example is of the 'communicating cactus'.

During a workshop on communication one of the participants commented, 'We have a boy in our class, John, who shows strange behaviour. If we are not careful, when John arrives in the morning, he picks up the cactus. Is it possible, looking at it from his viewpoint, that this is an attempt at communication?'

This was an interesting hypothesis. We asked, 'What happens when he does this? Does his behaviour provoke any interesting reaction for him?' 'Well, naturally the teacher runs straight over and tells him he shouldn't do it.' So John got a lot of attention for his cactus behaviour; it might have been negative attention, but negative attention was better than none. Maybe this was his way of saying good morning and we were wrong to be angry. We decided to teach him another way to get attention in the morning.

For three weeks a bell was put on John's work table, and every time he came in an adult led him away from the cactus and showed him how to ring the bell on the table. If he did this the teacher came to him, looking interested, and immediately gave him more, and, what is important, more positive attention than before. For three weeks, John was taught to ring the bell every morning. Finally a test situation was set up. Which did he choose: the cactus or the table bell? It was the table bell, of course. And it was good-bye cactus behaviour.

1.13. Communicate, yes, but with whom and where?

Once you have mastered a suitable form of communication and know the various functions of communication, you then must be able to use them with different people in a variety of situations. We have already explained that people with autism have difficulty with spontaneous generalization, and you can see this clearly in their communicative behaviour. Their preference for perceptual rather than conceptual information plays a major role.

One particular boy with autism was only nice to his teacher if she wore a blue ribbon in her hair. The rest of the time she was treated like a stranger, just like the others. Behaviour is connected to a perceptual detail. The use of words and pictures can also be connected to details of observation: pictures are used with teachers but not with father, or with father but not with teachers, or not with brothers and sisters, or only in the speech therapy room or at the dining room table . . .

Here is a vivid example of this inflexible way of thinking.

During a practical training session our participants noticed that Tom, a deaf boy with autism, liked to be tickled when in the free-time area, but he had no way to say so. Usually he communicated with cards, but there wasn't a card for 'tickling'. An excellent teaching objective was then developed from this. The students wanted to teach Tom how to ask to be tickled so they developed a communication card (two gently twitching hands: tickle)

During the next free-time period Tom was surrounded by a group of students who waited for him to show them the tickle card. But he didn't ask. Didn't he understand the card? They thought he did; he had been tested. Everyone was disappointed. What had gone wrong? Then one student noticed all the other communication cards were hanging from Tom's belt. We were confronted with an extreme example of problems with context. Tom had been given the tickle card directly; it had not been hung with the other communication cards on his belt. Because it was not in context with the others, Tom did not understand that the tickle card was a communication card. As soon as it was put with the others, he laughed and immediately showed his card 'Tickle me'.

To get a picture of the problem of context, we assessed the forms and functions of communication in various environments. It will not come as much of a surprise that young people with autism communicate best in surroundings where they are best understood, where they feel most comfortable and which are most adapted to their needs. It is even less surprising to hear that in different environments people with autism should be approached in a coherent way and that a child may face unnecessary problems when there is no well-coordinated policy.

One often finds that the professionals in classrooms and boarding schools do not work together effectively. That may not be so bad for mentally retarded children but for children with autism it is a disaster. One often sees children in an autism class (where there are specially trained teachers) asking for attention, food and drink with cards, while in the evening at boarding school, they revert back to stereotypes, throwing tantrums if they need something. Instead of showing cards, they will writhe on their stomachs. At the boarding school the professionals complain, 'Of course they have behaviour problems, they work far too hard in the class.' Classroom teachers reply, 'Of course they have so many behavioural problems: your environment and approach aren't suited to them.' A problem of context? Certainly, but one often caused by inadequate coordination, because in some places, boarding school, class and family all work together successfully and those children are much happier.

2. From theoretical understanding to educational intervention

2.1. The educational model of retarded development is not appropriate for people who have a different cognitive style

The communication problems of people with autism cannot be explained solely by a lower mental age. Many communication problems are connected to their cognitive style, so different from that of normal children, which has logical but far-reaching consequences for their education: if we understand that they are different, we must try to help them in a different way.

I am not talking only about teaching communication in the strict sense of the word, but about teaching every crucial subject in preparation for as meaningful a life as possible. Imagine an adult with autism learning to lay the table. Teaching like this works by imparting certain expectations that one hopes will be understood. In other words, communication.

The same goes for other lessons. Your individualized educational objectives must be understood by the child. Whether you offer physical help, or help through pictures or words, it still comes down to communication that at a certain level has to be appropriate.

2.2. Mixed classes. Suitable or unsuitable for people with autism?

The concept of mixed classes in special education has changed radically in Flanders during the past few years. Some 10 years ago one found children with autism in classes set up for mentally retarded who were not autistic. That was considered a mixed class. The children with autism were expected to adapt to the teaching methods and curriculum set up for the mentally retarded. This proved very difficult if not impossible. If the teachers said it was going well, they usually meant it was going well for themselves and that there were not too many behaviour problems. But there was usually no room for a really active individualized preparation for adulthood.

Since then the concept of a mixed class has changed: even if there are only two children with autism in a particular school, a class will often be set up which takes maximum account of their specific needs. As they are the weakest and most vulnerable, a special class is set up for them that makes them feel secure. Other children also benefit from such an arrangement. People are now thinking that there are other children in the school who have not been diagnosed as autistic but have similar disabilities (for example, children who also have difficulties in analysing meaning) and they may also benefit from these educational strategies. This new combination, in which the weakest do not have to adapt to the teaching methods and curriculum of the strongest, has more chance of success.

Over the past 10 years, there has been a growing awareness that children with autism really can make progress in learning provided that their education is adapted to their particular handicap. They not only learn in an adapted situation, in a one-to-one relationship, but they can also work both independently and sometimes with others (if the educational objectives are sufficiently individualized). Practice has also proved that this style of education, much more focused on visual clarity, is not only good for children with autism, but also for many other children who are not strictly diagnosed as autistic.

2.3. Not only simplify, but also create extra clarification

In the last chapter I described the cognitive problems of people with autism as a combination of retarded development and a different development. Most people with autism are mentally handicapped; they develop more slowly than normal – this is a quantitative aspect. However, autism is also 'different' – this is a qualitative aspect.

On the simplest level you might say that the most important educational strategy for mentally handicapped children is to simplify. Expectations are communicated in a simple way according to their development age. Simplification is also essential for children with autism, but different qualitative aspects of autism demand extra clarification.

An adult with autism once commented, 'You say that we have no empathy, but it's just the other way around. If you talk to me, you act as if you're the same as me. But I know that you are different.'

2.4. Visual thinkers need visual support

At the European conference at The Hague, another adult with autism, Temple Grandin, said:

> All my thinking is visual. When I think about abstract concepts such as getting along with people I use visual images such as the sliding glass door. Relationships must be approached carefully otherwise the sliding door could be shattered. As a young child I had visualizations to help me understand the Lord's Prayer. The 'power and the glory' were high-tension electric towers and a blazing rainbow sun. The word 'trespass' was visualized as a 'No Trespassing' sign on the neighbour's tree. Some parts of the prayer were simply incomprehensible. The only non visual thoughts I have are of music. Today I no longer use sliding doors to understand personal relationships, but I still have to relate a particular relationship with something I have read – for example, the fight between Jane and Joe was like the U.S. and Canada squabbling over the trade agreement. Almost all my memories relate to visual images of specific events. If somebody says the word 'cat', my images are of individual cats I have known or read about. I do not think about a generalised cat.

It might be pointed out that the statement above refers to a high-functioning person with autism, but these characteristics are certainly also present in 'lower-functioning' individuals, only then the situation is more complicated, because 'pure' autism is mixed with mental retardation, i.e. a 'slow' development.

2.5. Dyssymbolism

People with autism are like people with aphasia, 'dyssymbolic' with regard to what they hear: they have specific difficulties analysing the meaning of abstract auditory information.

With a congenital dysphasia it is known that the difficulties in the sphere of meaning analysis can be put down to a dysfunction of the left temporal lobe. Everyone finds it perfectly normal to present children with dysphasia communicative information in a way they find easier – via visual channels. It is difficult for them to adapt to us so we have to work harder to adapt to them.

Children with inborn development dysphasia are not specifically disturbed in their analysis of the abstract visual information that is part of our social behaviour. Children with autism on the other hand have difficulty not only in 'hearing beyond' the literal information (and here we can help them with visual support), but also in 'seeing beyond' the information given. They are dyssymbolic visually as well, and we must ask ourselves whether we are doing enough at this level to adapt to their handicap. The following anecdote explains how helpful visual support can be:

'Once upon a time' (but this is a true story) a 14-year-old deaf autistic boy was allowed to catch a plane to the Olympic Games for the disabled. He went in a jumbo jet and fell in love with planes of every size and colour. At the bottom of his work schedule there was a plane. He often picked it up in his free time and gazed at it from every possible angle, just like a lover. It was moving to watch him but sad at the same time. His range of actions with that plane were so limited. He never got further than a 'brum brum' noise, letting it take off and fly some 50 centimetres before landing. Even in moments of deep passion he remained locked in his lack of initiative, lack of purpose, lack of direction.

During a practical training session a group of students came up with the idea of visualizing other things he could do with the plane. A circuit 40 metres long was drawn and stuck in the free-time area to show that the plane could take off and land not only in the 50 centimetres in front of his eyes, but also around the entire perimeter of the recreation room. This was shown to him in a very explicit way. The result was predictable but astonishing nevertheless. He seemed to be truly released. He began to wave his arms, he took his plane, ran around the entire circuit, jumped up and down and ran around again. Visual support!

If we accept that people with autism are visual learners, why don't we call the autism approach simply an approach with visual support instead of 'structured education'? After all, this is what it is: if advice is asked on autism education in a class or group home, this is the first thing that comes to mind – which visual aids are used here?

I would propose no longer calling autism education 'structured' because the word 'structure' is too generalized and does not suffi- ciently emphasize the specific line of the approach. So many other forms of education are called 'structured'. What is the difference?

Moreover, the term 'structure' gives the wrong idea to outsiders. It sound as if structure were something enforced, something people have to adapt to: structure as the goal rather than structure as a means.

The term 'visual aids' makes it immediately clear that the means are there to help the child. It is a more 'social' word for the 'social' sector. Linguists have a good name for communication with visual aids: augmentative communication (augmentative meaning additional, supportive, increasing). With this analogy we can also call autism education 'augmentative education'.

2.6. The first letters of the autism alphabet

The problem with augmentative education is that many teachers not sufficiently educated in autism confuse the starting point with the final goal. We in Flanders and the Netherlands see this as only the very first step in the autism approach, while others see it – wrongly – as the end product.

ABC are the first letters of the alphabet; the work table, the work and the daily timetables are the first letters of the autism alphabet. Not the final goal, not a goal in themselves, but a means to achieve something more complete. With these aids pupils with autism find (sometimes for the first time) that their life is not dominated by coincidence, but that a link exists between an object and the activity that follows, that a visual symbol can mean something. And so they learn the first letters of a 'visual' alphabet, a 'visual' language that can later be used to communicate all sorts of expectations in a way they can understand and to teach them to cope on their own, including doing tasks such as housekeeping. (Figures 3.2 – 3.4)

2.7. Not an aim in itself but a means to greater independence. A review with perspective.

To repeat: this is the basis, not the final aim, of the autism approach.

- A daily timetable gives visual answers to the questions, 'WHERE and WHEN do I do something?'
- The work schedule gives a visual answer above all to the question: 'HOW LONG do I do this?'
- Next, all sorts of visual aids give an answer to the questions 'HOW do I organize my work?' and 'HOW do I carry out my task?' Finally, we offer activities that are clear in and of themselves, so that no more meaning is added than the pupil is able to cope with.

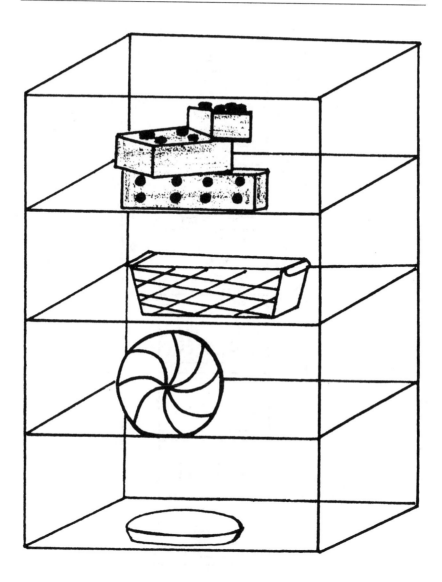

Figure 3.2. Timetable with objects

This is quite an accomplishment: being able to explain visually to people who have such difficulty giving visual concrete answers to rather abstract questions like 'what', 'where', 'how much' and 'how'? Yet I can understand how people who see only the work table and the daily timetable and cannot place these elements within a total perspective might feel that these leave an artificial and inflexible impression. Nevertheless, the origin and the result must not be confused. These are not inflexible teachers at work, but flexible

Figure 3.3. Timetable with pictures

teachers who are adapting to inflexibility, to another way of thinking of people with autism. Helping those who suffer from a lack of imagination requires vast imagination.

It must be remembered that those with autism learn only the first letters of the visual aids alphabet at the work table. That occurs through work skills such as sorting, packing, etc., i.e. the simplest tasks, which can be considered to 'speak for themselves'. Later, similar aids will be used for other kinds of job and in an environment other than the workplace. However, one begins by working in a situation that is easier for those with autism. Because for them, it is hard.

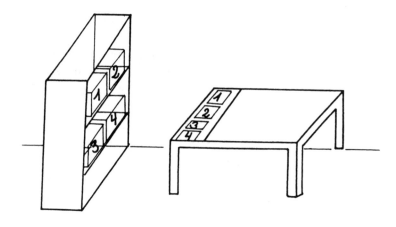

Figure 3.4. Work schedule

2.8. Visual support and 'augmentative education' as a means of release

Visual support can free people with autism from some of their basic problems: abstractions and following time sequences. The example that I like to give is to remind you of learning to drive a car. In the same way that washing oneself is a broad vague act for some people with autism, the idea of 'driving a car' was too broad and vague for us at the time. The instructor had to divide the task into steps that could be done consecutively. First, put the key into the ignition, then turn on the engine, then put the car into the right gear . . . He explained things step by step, we understood his language, and his verbal instructions served as a verbal support for our actions.

I think it is important to realize that even people with autism who are verbal have problems with 'verbal support'. In normal development we see that first echolalia and then verbal language are used for the purpose of self-regulation, to facilitate various actions. Later, verbal language is internalized, and this inner language helps us to regulate our actions. There are numerous indications that the process – even the people with autism who are verbal — does not work in this way. For people with autism, speech is often more complicated than their actual understanding, so this poor understanding – this poor inner language – rarely functions as a support for their actions. Visual support is, then, essential.

The augmentative systems, the systems of visual support, are those they will use as a means of release, to compensate for a number of basic problems inherent in autism. To sum up:

1. That which is too abstract can be made concrete via pictures, outlines or objects that have a lower abstract level and are therefore less remote than what is literally seen, the basic problem for people with autism. This is always true: the most abstract level is not usually the best, the best level is the level that they can handle independently.

2. In this way you can communicate things which cannot be understood otherwise. For them, that is real communication. Speaking is silver but making something visible is gold.

3. Visual aids teach people with autism to cope with change, making their thinking more flexible. It is easier to accept change if you can visually anticipate it. Often change is not the problem, it is the impossibility of anticipating it.

4. These visual aids heighten the level of independence.

5. The more independent they are, the fewer failures they experience and the fewer behavioural problems they have.

6. The fewer the stereotyped patterns of behaviour, thanks to their greater active involvement, the more normal people with autism appear and the greater the chance they have of social integration.

7. The fact that people with autism are less dependent on others to do various tasks brings other advantages (sometimes difficult for some teachers to accept). Often they are so dependent on one particular person for help that it is a disaster if the person leaves or their environment changes. If they can achieve a greater degree of independence with visual aids, the visual aids can be taken with them and a change of environment is less disastrous.

8. Sometimes those with autism are 'lost in time'. By actually seeing what the intermediary steps are, not only are the problems of conceptualizing solved, but also those of sequentialization – running through the various intermediary steps within a framework of time.

9. With this, many can escape a major problem – passivity – which often arises out of a lack of aids for self-regulation (their verbal memory is underdeveloped).

Additions can, of course, be made to the list above.

Finally, are people in an autism class (or living group) more able than other autistic people in a non-specialized environment? No. However, their skills are more functional because in an autism class or group, visual aids are used which they understand rather than verbal aids which offer them little support.

Chapter 4
Social interactions

My daughter Jessica, the youngest of my four children, at 25 could easily be presented as a competent adult. Jessy has a part time job in a college mailroom; she pays taxes. She cleans houses, irons, sews, and cooks, responsibly and well. She paints exact, finely rendered, subtly coloured acrylics, many of which have been exhibited and sold. She lives at home as a contributing member of her family. Her WAIS IQ 2 years ago was 106 (Verbal 98, Performance 116); on the Advanced version of the Raven Progressive Matrices Test, a test of exact observation and logical inference, she scored well above the 95th percentile, higher than all but a tiny fraction of university graduate students. All this being true, why shouldn't I make the claim every parent of a handicapped child dreams of – that she is normal?

Yet you would not have to exchange more than one sentence with her – indeed, you would not have to do more than observe her in a single social interchange at home, at work, or on one of her frequent shopping expeditions – to realize that all of these accomplishments, accomplishments that once seemed in the unreachable realm of miracle, do not add up to the expected sum: a human being fully comprehending of, and thus self-sufficient in, the daily life surrounding her.

Clara Park, 1986

1. Theoretical understanding

1.1. Being 'autistic'

It was just such a social characteristic (social isolation) that impelled Leo Kanner to call the 11 children he had been observing in his clinic over a period of 5 years 'autistic', saying that they were suffering from 'infantile autism' with autistic disturbances in their ability to have affective contact with others He noted that this social isolation was present from birth:

> We must therefore accept that these children came into the world with an inborn inability to have normal, biologically determined affective contact with people.

79

Kanner later wrote that this social isolation should not be seen as too definitive, that it was possible to determine a pattern of development in social behaviour and that many children with autism eventually did become interested in other people:

> Schizophrenics try to solve problems by retreating from the world but our children begin slowly to find compromises by carefully sending out feelers to a world in which they were originally total strangers.

The word 'autism' continues to cause confusion because, in spite of all the recent publications and all the scientific evidence, many people continue to associate the syndrome of autism with one symptom: withdrawal. Nevertheless, those who read the definition of autism carefully will come to the conclusion that withdrawal is a possible but not necessarily essential characteristic in a diagnosis of autism.

G., a 33-year-old adult with autism, who still lives with his parents, waits for the postman every morning. He always wants to kiss him, on the lips. He cannot be accused of being withdrawn (autistic) in the emotional sense of the word. His problem is more one of cognitive loneliness. He likes people and now that he is grown up he is even more motivated than before to act as others do. But he has problems understanding why people kiss, when they do it and how ...

Many people with autism are not withdrawn any more but they continue to suffer from 'being alone'. It was exactly this characteristic that lead me to study autism. I knew of loneliness from literature and from my own life, but I felt that loneliness in autism was something else altogether, something which far exceeded the usual emotional meaning of the word. It seemed to have more to do with a search for meaning in the chaos of experience and it was coupled with an 'intellectual' loneliness. I found it both horrifying and fascinating at the same time, and I wanted to understand more of such 'metaphysical' loneliness.

Luckily, the days when parents were made scapegoats for their children's loneliness are long past, but this idea virtually crippled research for 40 years. It took the research of Hermelin and O'Connor to rectify the situation by helping us to understand that social behaviour demands considerable flexibility and abstract insight with which an inflexible cognitive style cannot cope. Here, even more than in other areas of life, one must have the ability to rise above the 'literal' and to make more sense of things than pure perception alone allows. In fact we should not be surprised that although some better functioning individuals with autism initially make a normal impression when speaking, they later make obvious mistakes in social situations, because this is infinitely more complicated.

> I find it very difficult to grasp social things and will only succeed in most cases if every tiny step, rule and ideal is written down and numbered one after another in a column, then I have to go over these ever so many times in order to learn all these rules. But even this is no guarantee that you will always know how, when and where to apply things, as circumstances which are in any way different to how you learnt the rules will confuse. Some people have tried to teach me social things by linking similar ideas together, but this does not always work because the ideas seem to merge so that it is very difficult to differentiate which is which and how, when and where to apply these things because no one situation is identical to every other situation. I am afraid I have no good suggestions on how social things can be learnt. All I can say is that I prefer them to be written down in a column and numbered, but this is not likely to be of much value unless the autistic person can read – though I presume pictures portraying every little step could be used, but even these can be difficult for an autistic person to understand.
>
> *Therese Joliffe et al*, 1992

Social interactions were once defined as 'abstract symbols in permanent movement'. In that sense language is more 'static'; the words at least stay the same. However, no social situation is ever exactly repeated. The meaning of social interactions is hardly ever explicit; there is a constant need to analyse what one is observing for its true meaning.

1.2. 'Theory of mind' and social blindness

One aspect of the difficulties people with autism have with social interactions is illuminated in the 'theory of mind' hypothesis of Uta Frith and her colleagues. In her book *Autism: Explaining the enigma*, she has reproduced a painting by Georges de la Tour (Figure 4.1). Look at it carefully and try to understand its meaning before you read further.

You immediately see that people are playing cards. You also see that some cheating is going on. Look at the two ladies in the middle – their posture and look suggest a conspiracy. They have hatched a plot together to win the game. But they're also a bit too eager and undisciplined when it comes to cheating. I'm sure the rest of the party has seen through them. They certainly know what's going on,

Figure. 4.1. *The Cheat with the Ace of Diamonds* by Georges de la Tour, Musée du Louvre, Paris, reproduced by kind permission of Photographies Giraudon.

but no-one really cares. Look at the player on the left. He has a better plan than the two ladies. He's showing his cards (behind his back) to an onlooker out of sight. There is also the player on the right, the so-called 'introvert'. He'll win of course. He is looking at his cards very innocently, but surely he is the snake in the grass.

Is that the way you see it? Or do you have another interpretation? It doesn't really matter. What does matter is that you are able to guess what is going on in their minds. To format this rather abstractly: by observing the outward appearance of things, we try to guess at the inner meaning. We know that we can read behaviour and faces and make hypotheses about what people are thinking, feeling, planning. In other words we have a 'theory of mind'; we know there are emotions and intentions hidden behind what we see literally.

Reality to an autistic person is a confusing, interacting mass of events, people, places, sounds and sights. There seem to be no clear boundaries, order or meaning to anything. A large part of my life is spent just trying to work out the pattern behind everything. Set routines, times, particular routes and rituals all help to get order into an unbearably chaotic life. Even when I want sometimes to take part in something, my brain just will not tell me how I should go about it, and contrary to what people may think, it is possible for an autistic person to feel lonely and to love somebody.

Normal people, finding themselves on a planet with alien creatures on it would probably feel frightened, and would not know how to fit in and would certainly have difficulty in understanding what the aliens were thinking, feeling and wanting, and how to respond correctly to these things. That's what autism is like. If anything were suddenly to change on this planet a normal person would be worried about it if they did not properly understand what this change meant. That's what autistic people feel like when things change. Trying to keep everything the same reduces some of the terrible fear. Fear has dominated my life. Even when things are not directly frightening I tend to fear that something horrible might happen, because I cannot make sense of what I see. Life is bewildering, a confusing, interacting mass of people, events, places and things with no boundaries. Social life is hard because it does not seem to follow a set pattern. When I begin to think that I have just started to understand an idea, it suddenly does not seem to follow the same pattern when the circumstances alter slightly. There seems to be so much to learn. People with autism get very angry because the frustration of not being able to understand the world properly is so terrible – sometimes it gets too much. Then people say they are surprised when I get angry.

As it was a long time before I realized that people might actually be speaking to me, so it was a long time before I realized that I too was a person – if somewhat different from most others. I never thought about how I might fit in with other people when I was very young because I was not able to pick people out as being different from objects. Then when I did realise that people were supposed to be more important than objects and became more generally aware, things began to take on a new and more difficult light.

Therese Joliffe et al., 1992

People with autism have difficulty 'reading' emotions, intentions and thoughts. They are, to a large degree, 'mind blind', socially blind. They lack or have only an underdeveloped 'theory of mind'. In this sense Frith calls them strict behaviourists: an action for them is strictly an action, the meaning behind the action often eludes them.

They may seem to have no consideration for others, but it is not a question of emotional egotism, but rather a problem of cognitive inflexibility (their difficulty with the 'metaphysical'). In this sense they are the opposite of certain psychotics who see ideas and intentions behind everything (they have delusional ideas).

Thomas screams and yells enough to wake the entire street if, for example, I don't always let him get into the car on the same side or if I dress and undress him in the wrong order, if the place for something in the bathroom is changed, if I take a different route, if I don't buy 'green' coffee in shop X and batteries in shop Y, or if another ritual is broken.

I remember that after one particular awful day, I took Thomas to my room so that the other children could at least do their homework in peace. It was all too much for me and I burst into tears. Then I saw that little Thomas spontaneously began to crawl towards me.

I thought he wanted to comfort me and I started to cry even harder from happiness. Then he put his fingers to my eyes and started to laugh. It was the sparkling tears which fascinated him.

Hilde De Clecq

Here is yet another anecdote showing Thomas's 'social blindness':

If he's been eating too many sweets and I say that they're all gone and then he finds some, he says, 'You didn't look hard, did you?' or 'You didn't say that right, Mummy.'
Thomas doesn't really understand that I'm actually trying to tell him something.

1.3. Early social interactions with ordinary children and children with autism

It sounds paradoxical: the social interactions that give ordinary babies the most pleasure and satisfaction are those which threaten to cause the most irritation and need for isolation as a form of defence to babies with autism. The problem is not a diseased mother–child relationship as was once thought. It is simply a question of the different biological make-up of a baby with autism and, coupled with this, a different cognitive style. It is this which makes him react so strangely in our minds to the usual ways of expressing love – through language, smiles, cuddles and eye contact. It must be one of the worst things imaginable: a mother perplexed when her baby seems to refuse her love, who then seeks professional help, only to be told that it is her own fault. Let us sum up then the early social interactions of ordinary and autistic children. (Table 4.1)

1.4. Life as a stage. A person with autism on the football field of life

In their epidemiological research, Lorna Wing and her colleagues in Camberwell have signalled the existence of social subgroups in autism. They also point out that social characteristics can change, that children who first appeared to shut themselves off from the social world can 'thaw' and open up. Before we go into this study in detail, we will start with a simple analogy, an exercise in imagination that helps us to understand the various levels of social consciousness.

Our starting point is as follows. In order to understand social behaviour, we must intuitively take into account a huge number of invisible and unformulated rules. For example, when giving a lecture, a speaker looks at the public, he does not stand five centimetres away from someone, he does not always look at the same person, he modifies his tone to suit his subject, he knows the normal use of coffee breaks and takes account of that.

Table 4.1: Normal development

Age in months	Social interaction
2	Turns head and eyes to locate sound Social smile
6	Reaches in anticipation of being picked up Repeats actions when imitated by adult
8	Differentiates parents from strangers 'Give and take' object exchange games with adults Peek-a-boo and similar games with a script Shows objects to adults Waves bye-bye Cries and/or crawls after mother when she leaves the room
12	Child initiates games with increasing frequency Agent as well as respondent role in turn-taking Increased visual contacting of adults during play with toys
18	Peer play emerging: showing, offering, taking toys Solitary or parallel play still more typical
24	Peer play episodes are brief Peer play more likely to revolve around gross motor activity (e.g. chasing games) than sharing of toys
36	Learning turn-taking and sharing with peers Episodes of sustained cooperative interaction with peers Altercations between peers are frequent Enjoys helping parents with household chores Enjoys showing off to make others laugh Wants to please parents
48	Negotiates roles with peers in socio-dramatic play Has preferred playmates Peers verbally (and sometimes physically) exclude unwelcome children from play
60	More peer- than adult-oriented Intensely interested in forming friendships Quarrelling, name-calling with peers common Able to change role from leader to follower in peer play

Table 4.2: Development in autism

Age in months	Social interaction
6	Less active and demanding than non-handicapped infant
	A minority are extremely irritable
	Poor eye contact
	No anticipatory social responses
8	Difficult to soothe when upset
	About $\frac{1}{3}$ are extremely withdrawn and may actively reject interaction
	About $\frac{1}{3}$ accept attention but initiate little interaction
12	Sociability often decreases as child begins to walk, crawl
	No separation distress
24	Usually differentiates parents from others, but little affection expressed
	May give hug, kiss as automatic gesture when asked
	Indifferent to adults other than parents
	May develop intense fears
	Prefers to be alone
36	Failure to accept other children
	Excessive irritability
	Failure to understand meaning of punishment
48	Unable to understand rules in peer play
60	More adult than peer-oriented
	Frequently becomes more sociable, but interactions remain odd, one-sided

From: Watson, L. and Marcus, L. Diagnosis and assessment of preschool children. In Schopler, E. and Mesibov, G. (eds) *Diagnosis and assessment in autism*. London, Plenum Press, 1988

> Objects are frightening. Moving objects are harder to cope with because of the added complexity of movement. Moving objects which also make a noise are even harder to cope with because you have to try to take in the sight, movement and further added complexity of the noise. Human beings are the hardest of all to understand because not only do you have to cope with the problem of just seeing them. They move about when you are not expecting them to, they make varying noises and along with this, they place all different kinds of demands on you which are just impossible to under-stand. As soon as you begin to think you are grasping how one of them works, something happens to change all this.
>
> *Therese Joliffe et al., 1992*

From dawn to dusk there are thousands of rules important to social exchange. Life is like one long 'game' with rules and regulations far more complicated than those, say, of football.

Imagine that you are on a football field and you don't know any of the rules, but your team-mates expect you to join in . . . What would your reaction be? The situation might seem overwhelming, even frightening. You might then try to shut yourself off in any way you can – or cannot – from all the things going on, and to try to protect yourself from all the difficult people. If the players come too close and continue to insist that you play (using sounds you don't understand), you might even throw a tantrum. No, you can't do it. It is too complicated. You have no points of reference to get you started. You have enormous difficulties with physical and bodily contact. In this situation you would begin to resemble most the group of your people whom Lorna Wing calls 'aloof', the group who very nearly confirm the old clichéd idea of autism:

> I spent a great deal of my time alone in my bedroom and was happiest when the door was closed and I was by myself. I cannot remember ever thinking about where my mother, father, brother and sister were, they did not seem to concern me. I think this was because I did not for a time realise that they were people and that people are supposed to be more important than objects.
> I used to, and still want to, put a big dark blanket over my head. This desire increases when I am with unfamiliar people and in unfamiliar surroundings. Doing this makes me feel much safer.

> *Therese Joliffe et al., 1992*

Children who belong to this group often reach a higher level of social awareness later. One often sees a developmental growth much like that on the football field: after spending some time in the middle of all this activity (what are they doing?), your main fears are overcome. You don't really understand what is going on, but there is at least an awakening of interest. You start to look around more. You don't take the initiative (the game is too difficult for that), but if others come near you or touch you, it is less of a problem than before. Sometimes they even draw you into the game. Perhaps one puts a football in front of your foot while another gently pushes your right leg and you kick the ball. Hurrah, hurrah, everyone is happy. You have now taken part in the game to a certain extent. But as soon as the others stop insisting, stop taking the initiative for you, the interaction stops, although now you are ready to be a passive player in a simplified form of football. You have moved on to the second category of children with autism, the 'passive' group:

> One of the most striking things was that he was impossible to comfort. It seemed as if the presence of his mother or father didn't help him to experience a feeling of comfort or security. He also didn't (yet) feel the need to be picked up or cuddled. Brian was then three years old. He let himself be picked up and cuddled, but clearly didn't get anything from it. This was also apparent at his childminder's home. Her children were mad about Brian. You could really play with him. They couldn't imagine a better

living doll. When they were tired of him, they put him down, gave him his building blocks and he didn't bother them any more.

Cis Schiltmans

As the years go by you start to become more interested in your team-mates. You have now observed them for some time and you begin to understand and appreciate them better. They have made their evaluations and now don't ask too much of you; they have even started to take your preferences into account so they can reward you better. You begin to take more initiatives yourself during the game, especially as you now think you can understand it. In fact you think there are only two rules: run after the ball and, when you have the chance, kick it.

If you keep this up for two 45-minute periods, wildly running around and kicking, you will probably give the impression of being active but odd. Many people with autism belong to this 'active but odd' group. They want to do things as others do them, but they really can't (like the man who wants to kiss the postman on the mouth every morning).

Finally, there is one small subgroup who could be called 'nearly normal' They have made tremendous progress in life. Their use of language seems correct, and they seem to imitate social behaviour correctly; only now and again do they come up with inappropriate behaviour that one would not expect of someone of their level.

Let's stick to the football analogy a little longer. Ivan, a high-functioning adult, has been invited to be the goalkeeper in his football club. But to everyone's amazement he acts completely differently from the other times he has played in this position. He leaves the goal post. He swears at the referee. He shakes his fist at the other players. The referee finally sends him off the field. No-one understands what has got to him. And Ivan doesn't understand why the others are so cross with him. After all he has done his best.

Ivan had done some research for the second match. He had watched goalkeepers on television until he could imitate them perfectly. He had seen how one swore at the referee and he thought this was the right thing to do.

1.5. A triad of disorders: communication, social interaction and imagination

The division of young people with autism into 'aloof' and 'active but odd' comes, as we mentioned, from Lorna Wing. About 20 years ago she and Judith Gould began a study with far-reaching consequences for the education of young people with autism and associated disorders. She identified all the children in Camberwell under 15 years of age with motor, psychiatric, learning or behavioural disorders. The results showed that 21 children out of 10 000 from the same age group suffered from difficulties in the development of communication skills, social interaction skills and imagination together. That was a much larger proportion of young people than the usually accepted figures for those suffering from 'Kanner's syndrome' or 'classic autism': that applies to only 5 in 10 000. (According to Leo Kanner, the nuclear symptoms of autism were: (1) the inability of children to relate normally to people and situations from birth; (2) the development of complicated repetitive plans and activities; (3) a compulsive desire to preserve sameness.) The disorders in communication, social interaction and imagination are so often interconnected that they can be described as a triad. Children with this triad may find their entire pattern of interest dominated by repetitive stereotyped activities, which can persist for months or years.

Those of the children who were classified as aloof children had behaviour problems that showed little awareness. Their problems consisted in the main of tantrums, unpredictable biting, hitting or scratching, self-injury, pointless wandering, screaming, spitting or smearing. The stereotyped behaviour is usually simple and self-directed, such as looking at the movement of fingers, waving one's arms or swaying the body to and fro. The 'passive' children usually behaved the best as long as they could follow a trusted daily routine. Imaginative play was usually lacking or consisted of simply copying the activities of other children, for example feeding or bathing a doll. Their play lacked spontaneity and inventiveness; it was repetitive and limited in scope.

The 'active but odd' children had a mixture of socially directed behaviour disorders and problems that were connected to a lack of social awareness that puzzled parents and teachers. Many carried out repetitive activities such as building and rebuilding the same imaginary system of roads and bridges, or playing 'pretend games', for example such as being an inanimate object such as a train, an animal or a character from a television series. Repetitive routines with objects were usually later replaced by more abstract interests. The list of these possible interests was varied. It ranged from bus and train timetables, calendars, the family trees of royalty, physics and astronomy to particular species of birds or animals, even particular kinds of people. The interests were, in themselves, not abnormal; what made them abnormal here was the steadfast clinging to them,

with a lack of interest in anything else. The children had little or no
understanding of the practical use of these interests in everyday life.

Behavioural problems were common in this group. Repetitive
questions concerned socially unacceptable themes such as physical
defects or private details of people's lives.

> In the same way that I structured his environment and activities, I also had
> to teach him about the various categories of people and objects. He himself
> didn't see how things hang together. He would group pictures of bananas
> with people, cows with cars, people with animals and so on. I had to teach
> him everything. When he was over five years old, I was with him on the
> bus. All at once he saw a lady with an eye-catching hair style. He pointed at
> her and asked loudly, 'Mummy, is that a person or an animal?' I whispered
> in his ear that it was a person, a 'woman', a 'lady'. So then Thomas said,
> 'What's that standing on her head?'
>
> *Hilde De Clercq*

Oversensitive reactions sometimes result from criticism of socially
bizarre advances and these occasionally can become aggressive. A
small minority even come into conflict with the law. Lorna Wing told
me one story of a high-functioning adult with autism who took a toy
gun to the bank to get money. He had seen it done on television. Ten
police cars with screaming sirens were waiting to pick him up. He
didn't know he had done anything wrong: 'But that's the way you get
money from a bank!'

This sort of problem can occur because of an insufficient understanding of the social rules. It can lead to women being harassed
('everyone has got a girlfriend'). Sometimes it's connected to special
interests, for example taking a book on a favourite subject without
paying for it.

It is obvious that this classification into subgroups should not be
taken too strictly. Children can move from one to another. Characteristics from one group can also flow into another. One person
can even show the characteristics of different groups in different situations: for example he is active but odd at home, yet completely
withdrawn in an unfamiliar unstructured situation. It is with these
reservations that we include the following from Prizant, in which he
tried to list objectively the characteristics of Wing's and Gould's
social subgroups.

1. Social aloofness
    a. Aloof and indifferent in most situations (exceptions: having
       specific needs met)

    b. Any interaction is primarily with adults through physical means (tickling, physical exploration)

    c. Little apparent interest in social aspects of contact

    d. Little evidence of verbal or nonverbal turn-taking

    e. Little evidence of joint activity or mutual attention

    f. Poor eye contact, active gaze aversion

    g. Repetitive, stereotypic behaviours may be present

    h. May be oblivious to environmental changes (e.g. person entering room)

    i. Moderate-to-severe cognitive deficiency

2. Passive interaction

    a. Limited spontaneous social approaches

    b. Accepting of others' approaches

       – adult initiations

       – child initiations

    c. Passivity may encourage interaction from other children

    d. Little pleasure derived from social contact but active rejection is infrequent

    e. May be verbal or non-verbal

    f. Immediate echolalia more common than delayed echolalia

    g. Varying degrees of cognitive deficiency

3. Active-but-odd interaction

    a. Spontaneous social approaches are apparent

       – most frequently with adults

       – less with other children

    b. Interaction may involve repetitive, idiosyncratic preoccupation

       – incessant questioning

       – verbal routines

    c. Language may be communicative or non-communicative (if verbal), delayed and immediate echolalia

    d. Poor or deficient role-taking skills

       – poor perception of listener needs

       – no modification of language complexity or style

       – problems in shifting topics

    e. Interest in routine of interaction rather than content

    f. May be very aware of others' reactions (especially extreme reactions)

    g Less socially acceptable than passive group (active violation of culturally determined social conventions).

Wing's study also described children without autism and with appropriate social interaction, 'sociable' at least in comparison with the level of development appropriate for their age. They like social contact for its own sake, both with children and adults. A few of the children with this pattern of behaviour had a very low mental age, in some cases even under 12 months. They were often immobile, but had the same sort of pleasure in and response to social contact as a normal baby. They made use of eye contact, facial expression and gestures to show their interest, and made attempts to join in conversations. They contrasted sharply with the withdrawn group, as they paid attention when someone entered the room and anticipated social contact before it had actually taken place. Nevertheless, there was some stereotyped behaviour found even among some of the sociable children, usually those children whose language comprehension was under the 20-month level, who had not yet developed many 'pretend' games. Above that level the stereotypical behaviour at least did not dominate the entire pattern of behaviour: there was room for a variety of interests.

As we saw earlier Wing's study showed that the group of young people who suffer from the now familiar 'triad' disorders is much larger than was previously believed. The greatest number were found among the population of the severe-to-profound mentally retarded. Wing, however, says that she would probably have found a greater number of high-functioning persons with autism if children from normal schools had been involved in the study. Her research was added to by Steffenburg and Gillberg in Sweden, who found many more children with the 'triad' in the normal school population. This is Wing's conclusion: 'children with the triad of social, communication and imagination disorders are perhaps born without, or with only a limited, capacity to understand and produce the normal type-specific sounds . . . They also lack the skill to perceive the environment and to form complex understandings concerning the environment, and to realise that human beings are extremely important and potential partners in a process of social exchange.'

This has serious social consequences for the development of two-way social interaction, the understanding and use of verbal and non-verbal communication and symbolic 'pretend' games. The typically repetitive behaviour of children with autism is perhaps a substitute for routine and goal-directed activities:

> His questions had to do with whatever he was fixated on at the moment: What time is it? (even though he knew quite well how to tell time). How deep is this water? How far does this hole go? How big is this? But our

answers rarely, if ever, satisfied him. We tried to show him, if possible, but that never worked either; it was as if he wanted something else, something more, but we couldn't make out what it was.

He asked the same questions over and over, thousands of times. He had no regard for where we were or for what we were doing. Sometimes when we'd say, 'You know the answer to that,' he'd giggle, other times he'd explode in anger. We knew his questions came from anxiety, from some fear. But of what? We had no idea how to give him any relief . . .

It was apparent that he needed to control conversations. Since he didn't seem to understand what other people said, he tried to force all of us to take part in his own rituals. It was lists, order, repetition.

Mrs Barron, 1992

1.6. The spectrum of autistic disorders (autism and related disorders). Towards an educational definition of autism

We now come back to one of our basic assumptions: people with autism have a different vision of reality, they have a biological defect in their ability to understand meaning behind what they see. They have a problem with imagination, they have difficulties going beyond the literal. They think more inflexibly and cannot sufficiently de-couple their mind from reality in order to be able to share our conversations, our social intercourse or our interests in the usual way.

Yet scientific research has shown that it is not exclusively children with 'autistic' problems who have difficulty making sense of things. With this in mind I spoke to Lorna Wing after a lecture in Antwerp, asking her whether she believed that there were children all over the world in special schools who would benefit from the autism educa-tion methods. She strongly confirmed that she did. Accordingly, all teachers who work with severely mentally retarded children should be given autism training.

When talking about autism-related disorders (or the autistic 'spectrum'), one must be aware that 'related' refers to the primary characteristics of autism (social interaction, communication, imagi-nation) and not the secondary related characteristics (e.g. hyperactiv-ity, attention deficit disorders, behavioural problems). The fact that people within this broad autism group suffer from qualitative impair-ments in the development of social interaction, communication and imagination, means that – in spite of individual differences – they need a similar type of educational approach tailored for people who suffer from autistic disorders in the strict sense of the word, an approach that is primarily rooted in strong individualization, visual support, predictability and continuity as they all comply with the educational definition of autism.

Lorna Wing herself spoke on this subject in a speech to the Dutch Parents Association (NVA):

> – if someone suffers from the triad – in any form – his personal development is seriously affected. People with this disorder find ordinary life difficult, confusing and frightening. They are vulnerable and escape into a range of activities that is limited in order to find safety and predictability. They need similar help with education, recreation and employment. They are dependent on others and must be supplied with an external framework in which structure and organization make their lives a little clearer and easier.

While the group with autistic disorders is, in the strict sense of the word, clearly defined ('The best validated child psychiatric syndrome' according to Rutter and Schopler), more scientific research is needed to define precisely that wider group within the autism spectrum. Half of the children diagnosed 'atypical' whom I saw last year had been wrongly given this label, probably to 'shield' the parents (autism is though to be such a 'cruel' diagnosis). Some parents do seem to find it easier to live with a diagnosis of 'atypical' or 'Asperger' (a term which is also used for high-functioning people with autism). I am an advocate of honest information. Yes, perhaps the name Asperger is better at indicating that the child can speak, can perform higher activities and use his imagination, is more interested in people than (again the clichéd image) those withdrawn into themselves or the more passive autistic child. But seen from an educational standpoint they are still 'autistic'. They have the same essential problems with imagination, social interaction and communication, even if at a higher level.

At the NVA congress in 1993 Lorna Wing said:

> It is justifiable for scientific researchers to look for specific sub-groups and to formulate strict criteria. But it is not justifiable to cut off children within the triad from certain forms of assistance, suitable special education because they do not conform to the classical definition of autism, when this is precisely the sort of help they and their families so badly need.

2. From theoretical understanding to educational intervention

2.1. The 'Harolds' are known in numerous institutions

Harold is a 40-year-old non-verbal man with a moderate mental handicap and autism. He suffers from autism, but all his life he has been treated as 'mentally ill'. He has spent many periods in psychiatric institutions but is now once again in a group home with mentally retarded adults without autism. He is the only autistic resident in his group home, where he has a very bad reputation because of his behavioural problems: extreme passivity at certain times or extreme dependence on any social worker nearby. Sometimes he just screams, hits, claws or tears the wallpaper off the walls. If the behavioural problems last very long, he is sent back to therapy for a while.

Although people with autism communicate in a different way from that of normal people, people still try to communicate with Harold verbally. They often think he has understood instructions perfectly well but is just being stubborn and doesn't want to communicate. Once he had a toy guitar, which he strummed on for hours, driving everyone crazy. It was taken from him; they were afraid that he otherwise would not do anything else.

Although social interaction is difficult for people with autism, the accent in the group home is put on group experience and group activities. Harold is usually happiest alone, but in the group home they think that he must learn to enjoy participating like all the others: 'otherwise he'll become more autistic than he already is'.

Harold is trapped in many social situations that are too difficult for him to handle. He is expected to live up to social expectations that he cannot fulfil. Because of his communication problems he is not able to say, 'This is too difficult for me.' His way of saying that it is all too much for him is clawing, screaming, biting, and tearing the wallpaper off the walls. This says it all: 'I can't go on, it's too difficult.'

There are many people like Harold. And professionals not trained in autism are only human. They can only cope for a few years – difficult for both sides – before they become fed up. If we look at the way in which Harold spends his day in the group home, we begin to understand some of the difficulties.

The afternoon is the best part of his day: he gets to spend 3 hours in the workshop with the unbelievable luxury of individual attention. Harold works then, but because he has not learned to use a visual plan (and this would be possible as he can easily recognize photos), he has to rely on his instructor for everything. He watches him and the instructor helps him, over and over again, every afternoon, a hundred times a day. Maybe Harold thinks it is expected of him to watch intently, that this is an essential part of the work. But with so little independence he is pretty helpless even at this, the 'best time' of his day.

It is lucky for Harold that the group home has a set routine as it means that he can predict the daily order of things; this gives him a feeling of security. But there are still weekends and holidays and other unpredictable changes that overwhelm him. This produces hand-biting. You should see the scars on his left hand. The professionals often try to involve Harold in the household activities, the washing, the washing-up, setting or clearing the table, but it isn't easy. A task such as setting the table may seem simple to us, but Harold does not understand all the steps it involves. He looks at the others and tries to copy them, but he often gets it wrong: too many plates, too few glasses, forks at the right instead of the left . . . He should really be able to 'see' what is expected of him, but instead he is given his instructions verbally. 'Set the table.' He sets off full of enthusiasm, but 5 minutes later he's staring into the void. That huge black hole of incomprehensions with no direction. He completely freezes. 'Look at him just standing there, the lazybones.'

Free time is the most difficult for Harold to cope with, and unfortunately there are over 8 hours of free time every day. Sometimes he was encouraged to sit around at the table playing cards with the others. Then he swayed to and fro. The proximity of all the others, the giggling and the activity that he didn't understand were unbearable. Luckily, the group leader quickly understood this: card-playing is out for Harold, and the other residents of the group home prefer playing cards without Harold anyway. Good . . .

But this doesn't solve the free-time problem for Harold. He wants to do all sorts of things in his free time, but he doesn't know what or how or where or for how long. He becomes eaten up by all his conflicting feelings of wanting something but not being able to do it. Then he screams or follows the professionals who don't know what to do with this extreme dependence ('go sit down like everyone else'). Sometimes it gets so bad he explodes: screams, bites, tears wallpaper . . . Harolds are found in lots of institutions. With the best of intentions and energy but without specialized training in autism and with small numbers of staff, the worst often happens. For years people do their best for him but finally it becomes impossible for everyone, both for them and for the Harolds. Then drugs are brought in to compensate for the lack of a specialized treatment for autistic people.

2.2. About 'negativism', lines of graduality and forms of social awareness

I think we must honestly accept that 'autism' is a negatively loaded word in traditional social work. Even so, young people with autism should only be accused of negativism in situations in which it can be proved that they actually refuse to comply with a request that they clearly understand. The presumption than an individual consciously chooses to refuse presupposes an important level of social and task involvement that is not often found in people with a severe handicap. The way in which a person with autism responds to the demands made upon him is fairly predictably connected to the difficulty of the task, the unfamiliarity of the situation, the person helping him and other similar factors.

The misconceptions surrounding negativism are first of all due to such things as unsuitable expectations, an unstructured environment and a poorly adapted social and communicative style. This is most often found in traditional 'integrated' surroundings where autism is not well understood. A lack of motivation and recalcitrance often disappear if the expectations and the tasks are adapted to the developmental level of the child. This sort of adaptation is an absolute must to ensure 'suitable' social behaviour.

We in the social sector have a certain tradition of dealing with communication difficulties. We are becoming more aware that there are 'higher' and 'lower' forms of communication. Talking is the finest form, and those who cannot talk can no doubt be helped via a 'lower' form of communication, for example pictures.

We know better than we knew before that play development does not occur by moving straight to fifth gear. We don't start with symbolic play right away; there are many kinds of simpler play that come first.

The concepts of 'higher' and 'lower' forms have up to now been less developed in terms of social interaction, probably because autism is unique in this area. As mentioned earlier, children with other kinds of handicap (mentally handicapped, blind, deaf, aphasic children) are not particularly limited in their ability to deal with social interaction.

Just as we associate talking (the highest form) with communication, we associate reciprocity (the highest form) with social interaction. We automatically assume that reciprocity must be present in everyone, even in people with autism because this is called for in all group situations. But in fact this is not so obvious. As an example let us look at an ordinary game played by two people in which there are not many social expectations, just respect for a few routine rules.

In Figures 4.2 - 4.6 you can see how in such social interactions much information is visualized, made concrete. Young people with autism can see exactly what they are going to do (bowl), where they have to stand (in the circle), how long the activity will last (the number of balls next to them) . . .

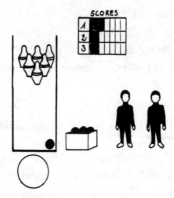

Figure 4.2: 1. Playing together, keeping score and having a winner . . . This is high-level play. Too high for people with autism.

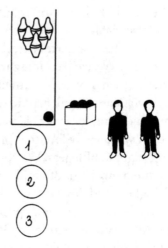

Figure 4.3: 2. One step down: waiting your turn while you play together. The circles on the floor make things clearer.

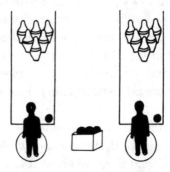

Figure 4.4: 3. Here the two players don't have to wait, but they must learn to share the same equipment.

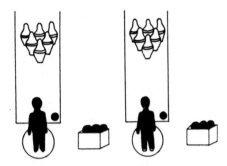

Figure 4.5: 4. Another step down: they are not really playing together but side by side. They both have their own equipment.

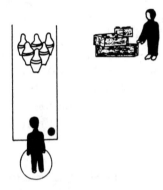

Figure 4.6: 5. This social level is high enough for certain people with autism: having someone else playing in the vicinity. Here they are not playing the game but they are playing near each other.

It immediately becomes apparent how important it is, especially in the area of social skills to develop an activity gradually, taking it in small steps.

2.3. An investigation into social skills

It seems strange that, 50 years after Leo Kanner, so little has been done in connection with the development of the social skills of autistic people. (This may have been because it was not a problem commonly found among handicapped people in general). For a decade time was wasted thinking that it was simply a problem of motivation – they can but they won't – or that it was the fault of the parents. Another important reason it was overlooked was the very complexity of learning social skills: isn't everything in our lives ultimately social; travelling, working, eating, sleeping – don't we do them all together? Where then does one begin?

In the TEACCH social curriculum the following social characteristics have been selected for observation: proximity, objects and
body use, social initiation, social response, interfering behaviour and
adaptation to change.

1. *Proximity*. Here observations are made about tolerance of bodily
   proximity. 'Direction' is another aspect of this: is someone looking
   at the right person when he is talking? Does he look at you if you
   speak to him? And does he understand which activities are carried
   out where (the recreation area for play, the work corner for work)?
2. *Objects and body use*. Does he have too many bizarre motor movements that will hinder later integration (continuing to walk on
   tiptoe, for example)? Does he understand that a spoon is to eat
   with and not to make noises with?
3. *Social response*. How does he react if others smile or say hello?
   When his brother asks him to play? Can he shake hands?
4. *Social initiation*. Can he say good morning himself in the mornings? That can be a very important public relations skill later, for
   work; these details can determine the attitude of an employer
   with regard to taking on a handicapped person. Can the autistic
   person explain that he is confused, doesn't understand something, that he doesn't have a fork or a spoon?
5. *Interfering behaviour*. Does he show aggression towards himself or
   others? Does he masturbate in public?
6. *Adaptation to change*. Does he still become upset when his
   programme or details in the environment change? Is he able to
   generalize skills and behaviours?

All these characteristics are observed in various situations relevant to
the lives of the majority of young people with autism: structured
time, play/leisure, eating/mealtime, during travel, when meeting
others (Figure 4.7) Each level of independence is defined: resistance,
physical prompt, general prompt, specific prompt, independence.

Let us consider an example. Suppose you observe 'proximity' in
'structured time'. How do you now go about interpreting the level of
independence?

- A pupil comes into the class for the first time. He has not yet
  formed work habits; he finds it difficult to sit still. The teacher
  invites him to come to the work table but he doesn't understand.
  He cries and screams. He will not let anyone take him to the work
  table. He shows 'resistance'.

	Context proximity	Objects/ body use	Social initiation	Social response	Interfering behaviour	Adaptation to change
Structured time						
Play/leisure						
Travel						
Mealtime						
Meeting others						

Figure 4.7: Summarizing chart for observation and assessment of social skills

- Three weeks later. The teacher invites him to come to the work table. He still doesn't really understand. The move from one place to another is still difficult. But if the teacher physically leads him, giving him a gentle push in the right direction, he responds. He no longer shows resistance but he needs a physical prompt.
- Three months later. Now he begins to know the class routines, but it is still difficult for him to make a move completely independently. Now, however, if it's time to go to the work table, the teacher says so directly ('Work') or shows him the work table card. He goes, no longer needing physical guidance, but needing a specific prompt.
- A few months later. He doesn't need any direct encouragement at all any more. Indirect will do. If the teacher stands in front of him and says or gestures 'What do you do now?', he understands at once and goes on his own to the work table. To us this may seem a very small step forward, but for him it's a big one; now he must be able to work within a timeframe and make a decision. He only needs a general prompt. Cognitively this is a much greater task.

Now he is completely independent. He may have needed one more intermediate step to become as independent as when the teacher was nearby, but at last he understands that even if she is not there, he has to work independently. Independence is no longer tied to her. He has 'generalized'.

When drawing up a social programme we choose several priorities with teachers and parents. Indeed, every item on the plan is a possible priority: working on 'proximity' when eating (sitting still in one's chair), social initiatives when eating (not taking things from others' plates), and so on. The level of independence in each situation is then examined (for example, physical guidance) and the learning goal is established and set one step up the ladder of independence (in this case moving from physical guidance to direct encouragement).

Teachers who have used this social learning plan have come to the following conclusions:

1. The number of social difficulties you register after such thorough observation is impressive. Not because you have really discovered anything surprising (after all you have had the child in class for months), but because there are so many when you actually list them.
2. You realise that you have enough material for a 'social skills' programme for the student's entire life.
3. You get not only a better insight into social difficulties, but also a different point of view on autism.
4. The difference in the level of social skills between structured and unstructured situations is noticeably large. It makes you aware of where the child is most comfortable.
5. It is very encouraging to talk to the parents about social priorities. You learn to appreciate their viewpoint, and their realization that there are other children in the class apart from their own starts to grow.
6. Thanks to these objective facts you at least know what you are talking about with colleagues and parents. Parents often complain that the reports are almost interchangeably vague. It is going 'well' or 'better', 'he has made (a little) improvement', and so on. With this sort of evaluation system you learn to work in steps. That makes your work more interesting, less exhausting than when your expectations were too high.
7. You learn to see what mistakes you would have made had you been over ambitious and not worked in steps.

2.4. Someone with a pervasive disorder also needs 'pervasive protection'. Notes on integration, normalization and segregation

Here are two witnesses who speak for themselves:

> I hated school. Parents of autistic children should never think about sending their children to ordinary schools, because the suffering will far outweigh any of the benefits achieved. The children just cannot tell anybody they are suffering and if you do end up with A-levels it does not

really make people want you, so it seems that you cannot use qualifications to obtain, let alone keep, a job. Although ordinary schooling enabled me to leave with a dozen or so O-levels and a few A-levels and then to obtain a degree, it was not worth all the misery I suffered.

The teachers pretended to be understanding but they were not. I was frightened of the girls and boys, the teachers and everything there. I was frightened of the toilets and you had to ask to use them which I was not able to do, also I was never sure when I wanted to go to the toilet anyway and the teachers got fed up with having to take me to the nurse to change me. It was mainly the women who were horrible, the men were a bit nicer. When I was at school I was kicked, hit, pushed over and made fun of by the other children. When I attended a place for autistic children, life was a little more bearable and there was certainly less despair.

However, once at university I was rarely teased, let alone kicked. I was allowed always to sit in my favourite places and when it came to my exams I was separated from the others in my favourite room, with the conditions as I like them, because any change from my usual timetable was found to have an adverse affect on my work. I ended up with a high upper second degree.

Therese Joliffe et al., 1992

In the new school we had 17 subjects in the first year. That was a lot. There were about 1,300 pupils and about 150 teachers and head teachers. Don Bosco was a saint who founded a school for clever and not so clever children. The boys at Don Bosco teased me because I asked lots of obsessive questions which concerned unreality, e.g. they told me 'I'll set your house on fire. My car can go three hundred kilometres per hour. I'll give you five punches back in the face if you give me one.' I worried about this a lot, and I believed everything they said. On a Tuesday in December 1979 a boy gave me a kick by accident. Then I kicked the boy with my feet against his legs and then he gave me two hard punches in my face. My teeth were hit a bit crooked and my mouth was bleeding seriously. I and the other boy had to go to Mr. Van Leuken who was the priest in the chapel and headmaster at the same time. After a few weeks my face healed. When it was Christmas at Granny Diedie's I asked my cousin a stupid unreal if-question. He said 'If you hit me once, you'll get one back in your face.' When I heard that I worried too much about it. When I was worried, I hit Bob a few times and then he gave me the same number back and I began to cry and worried about it for a few weeks. After that it was all over . . . The year at Don Bosco school didn't go very well because I had problems getting along with people every day.

Maarten Jonckheere

The concerns above and the story that follows make a modest contribution to the debate on the correct approach to use generally with people with autism and particular with high-functioning people with autism and those with 'atypical autism'. In the light of the diagnostic confusion that still reigns here and there, it should be pointed out that Therese Joliffe and John (whose story follows) would be labelled 'atypical' by some diagnosticians. However, even if they are 'atypical', they are people with a 'pervasive development disorder', and need just as much protection and help in integrating. Protection comes first. Words such as 'normalization,' 'integration', 'main-streaming', and more recently 'inclusion' have become popular. All refer to the rights of people with autism – which are the same as those of normal citizens and should include the right to an appropri-ate education. The normalization movement originally began in Scandinavia, where the aim was to let handicapped people live and work in 'the least limiting environment'. If you take the Scandina-vian concept of 'the least limiting environment', the debate takes a different turn and one does not think immediately of 'normal educa-tion' but rather of a form of special education (Mesibov, 1990): education in an autism class (segregation) or in 'mixed classes'. Thanks to such concerns about 'the least limiting environment', many handicapped people were removed from large institutions where nurs-ing and protection were more important priorities than the maximum possible degree of independence. However, over years of discussion I have had the impression that at some point the means and the goal became confused. The 'integration politics' were seen as an end in themselves and not as a possible medium- or long-term goal.

As Gary Mesibov writes, the heartfelt discussions increasingly became based more on moral principles (the 'good' (for integration) versus the 'bad' (against integration)) than on objective scientific facts. To illustrate this the story of 'John' follows. John is a boy with autism 'with normal intelligence', a composite invented from discus-sions and questions asked of parents, children with autism, teachers, social workers and experts. 'John' was created out of all this material. He is now 20 years old and will finish his secondary education at a Flemish school. The experience of John, his parents, his fellow pupils, his various teachers and social workers would be enough to fill a number of voluminous books. They are stories of insecurity, doubt, despair, loneliness and fear, but also of hope and great expec-tations. Above all they are stories of determination and persever-ance. John's life at nursery school, primary school and secondary school will be regularly interrupted for further observations on 'inte-gration'. The story is by Etienne Van Oosthuysen (1986), who wrote it at my request for a conference on education:

> When John was three, he was able to start nursery school. His parents kept
> their fingers crossed: he was toilet-trained but often difficult, he cried a lot,
> often didn't understand what was said to him and hardly talked. His
> mother was often exhausted in the evening because she had been so busy

with John. She was very relieved that he would be spending his days in school; it was a burden lifted from her shoulders.

But she was also worried (and felt guilty) about inflicting such a burden on the nursery school teacher. With John among 25 other small children things could get out of hand. His mother knew how much energy John required. For this reason she didn't dare talk to the head teacher about his problems when she enrolled him. His father and mother hoped that being with other children in the class and playing games with the nursery teacher would calm him down.

He began going half days. When he came home at lunch he was often overly excited; he cried even more than usual, rushed around the house causing havoc, didn't eat and was quiet only when he went to sleep. 'It's still early,' said his parents. 'He'll get used to it.'

But after a month had passed both the nursery teacher and the parents needed to talk. The teacher explained that John was good at puzzles and was intelligent, but his behaviour was very destructive, he didn't seem to understand when he was told to do something, never played, walked aimlessly around the classroom, and acted as if he were alone in the room. Moreover, the teacher complained that she had to spend too much time keeping an eye on him.

By Christmas the parents were asked to visit the headmistress. She declared that John was not 'normal', she talked of 'hyperactive children' and said that John was 'demanding'. She said he was 'spoilt' and 'got his way too much at home', she spoke of psychologists and even psychiatrists. She even asked if John's hearing was normal. His parents were now very concerned. Their GP sent John to a 'psycho-medical' centre. The therapist who evaluated John at the centre suggested 'a firmer more responsible' approach and said that he had the feeling that John was spoilt. The intelligence test showed a 'normally functioning child'. The parents were greatly relieved by these last results but the rest left them deeply confused, frightened and full of questions. What was the matter with John? The psycho-medical centre had recommended 'behaviour-therapy principles' – in other words, good behaviour was to be rewarded and bad behaviour punished. This didn't help. Indeed it produced just the opposite results. John seemed to become even more disturbed. The family hardly ever visited the grandparents for they were not able to cope with John and they too accused him of being spoilt. When his parents took him with them to do the shopping, they knew the gossip began the minute they left the shop; his mother had already experienced this often. Visitors made John worse and this always caused problems. Soon people stopped coming altogether.

At school things were much the same as they had been the very first year. At Easter however his teacher fell ill and John became terribly upset when a substitute took over. He had become a keen puzzle fan but with the new teacher he was more aggressive than ever, he cried more, didn't listen and started to bite other children. This was the last straw. Several parents rang the headmistress to complain that it was irresponsible to allow John to stay in the class with their children. 'Something has to be done!'

In May there was another visit to the headmistress. After making his first teacher ill, John was now victimizing his friends. It was agreed that

John should spend the rest of the school year at home and that his parents would take him to a child psychiatrist. They did this over the summer holidays. The diagnosis: John was autistic. The parents had never heard of this but the psychiatrist's voice made it clear that it was serious. The child psychiatrist proposed that they sent John back to his nursery school after the holidays. But both at home and at school there had to be a structured approach, a system of reward for good behaviour. The parents were full of great expectations. At the same time though they were very shocked by the diagnosis: that John was autistic. They understood that this was a serious developmental disorder, that it was incurable, that it demanded years of patience and a disciplined approach if his behaviour was to improve. They read all they could about autism. What they read was even more of a shock. John was seriously handicapped. The idea that John would be a burden for life was barely tolerable, almost unimaginable. But they knew that they had to struggle on with John.

Now we come to the second nursery school class and a new teacher who was both kind and idealistic. She wanted John in her class. John could stay in at break because the playground was too complicated and frightening for him. This helped. As arranged with the psychiatrist a special reward system was worked out for John to teach him to behave better and to stop crying, biting, kicking, screaming and wandering around in an unacceptable way. First a list was drawn up with the nursery school teacher showing all of John's disruptive behaviour. The teacher paid close attention to this. John was rewarded with cut-out bears in all colours. John worked to collect the bears, which helped. It also helped at home. John became quieter and a fanatic bear hunter. By Easter he had two jars full of bears. During the year he learned to sit still at his desk when pasting, doing puzzles or singing. The rest of the time he was still very wild. He still didn't talk much, he could form sentences but he often used the wrong words and continued to confuse 'I' and 'you'.

A new problem arose with the other parents. John got rewards (bears) while the other children didn't. During an inspection visit the school inspector indicated that the teacher's approach endangered the 'emotional climate' of the class because she paid so much attention to one child who clearly did not belong there.

In the third nursery class John had the same teacher. By now she could cope with John although it was still very exhausting. His speech was still backward. Social contact remained impossible. John kept to himself. In the tests to see if he was ready for primary school, John scored badly in concentration, vocabulary, ability to work independently and attention span. He did well on psycho-motor exercises, doing puzzles and anything to do with sums. It was expected that he would have major difficulties with the move to primary school. The disruptive behaviour, lack of concentration and inadequate use of language were seen as the main stumbling blocks. A small school prepared to accept John had to be found. It was also suggested that John be sent to an institute for special education with 'residential treatment'. His parents found this idea unacceptable.

The difficulties faced by all the main characters in this story are the result of what might be called a naive concept of integration.

Teachers, headteachers and inspectors with no previous training had no professional consultation services specializing in autism to fall back on, and they paid the price for this. (One motivated teacher was even forced to take sick leave because of the strain). There were enormous problems for John's parents: lack of understanding, insecurity, feelings of guilt. There were difficulties for the other children too; John got bears, they didn't . . . And of course the greatest anger and frustration was felt by John himself.

Occasionally, we go to Italy to give training courses. Integration there has been carried out with the utmost naivety, so much so that there are virtually no special schools left. All special children have been 'normalized' in normal education. Alberto is one such example of this. The first day of our practical training course, while we were waiting for our five pupils to arrive, Alberto strode triumphantly into the classroom with a car mirror in one hand and two broken window wipers in the other. His teachers followed him nervously, then delivered him into our hands, clearly wondering if they shouldn't stay longer in case we needed protection. Within the first 5 minutes Alberto had completely destroyed the workplace and thrown the well-prepared tasks into the air. Seventeen years old and fully integrated into normal education . . . In practice here is the way it really works. Day in day out Alberto has an adult who cares for him and accompanies him to his normal classes. This person has no training in autism. Every time Alberto becomes difficult his carer takes him out for a walk to calm him down. Alberto thus spends days at a time walking about so that he doesn't disturb the class. If he becomes difficult during walks – and this happens more and more often – his carer takes him home. Fully integrated? In what sense? Whose needs are being fulfilled here?

Back to John.

The next choice of schools fell on a small village school. It had three classes. He could walk to school with the neighbourhood children. When he was enrolled the headmaster had serious reservations. 'John can attend the school if he is able to adapt to it and not the other way around. After all, there's always special education.' (Everyone in the village knew John by then.) The parents realized that this wasn't going to be easy. It would all depend on the village teacher.

In spite of all this John had the capacity to learn. He was intelligent, but he had to be pushed. His parents stuck at it stubbornly. They went back to talk to the headmaster. They heard that the teacher couldn't cope with John any longer. The group must not suffer because of John's problems, they had to be able to learn. It was suggested that John return to the nursery school but they didn't want to take him back either. By now John was of compulsory school age. So back to primary school. The teacher agreed to try using behaviour modification principles with John. He was prepared to try but there were the other children to consider too. It was further agreed that maximum use would be made of the remedial teacher's aid. John would have six hours of lessons with him a week while the others had their language lessons. John was much calmer in the small classroom with its plain grey walls and a teacher all to himself. He was able to keep John's attention often, particularly if he used pictures to accompany the words. The first words John spoke at primary school were to the remedial teacher.

After two months John began to read separate letters, then words, and after a while, sentences. Modern mathematics went well. But the hours John spent with the rest of the class were less successful. He couldn't follow anything. The teacher's explanations weren't clear to him. John only took homework home which he had been given by the remedial teacher. Anything done with the whole class simply passed him by. The same thing happened with the nature walks; John hung behind the group. The teacher constantly had to keep an eye on him. John had no idea of the dangers of traffic. At the end of the first year John's report was unlike those of the other students. It consisted only of a report by the remedial teacher who praised John for his efforts.

He was advised to stay behind and repeat the first year again. And that is what he did. That second year John learned to read, again with the extra attention given him by the remedial teacher: such an individual approach brought results.

The learning process finally began. John continued to be isolated and still had outbursts of tears during the lessons but at home there was enthusiasm: a breakthrough had been made. John's results could now be translated into grades on his school report like those of his classmates. John began to understand that grades expressed appreciation for what he did at school. Above all it was his mother who made this clear through her enthusiastic reactions. John started to find grades important. An external learning motivator had been discovered. He spent several more years in primary school. It is impossible to describe them all in detail but let us look at some of the main issues.

John proved above all to be very good with figures. Division, multiplication, decimals were all child's play to him, although he couldn't understand word problems. Language continued to prove difficult. Technically he learned to read after four years of schooling, but spelling was still difficult. Reading comprehension was a disaster.

Thematic subjects (history, geography, nature study) were totally incomprehensible to him. He appeared to understand nothing of the world around him. He learned the necessary lessons off by heart but for him the world around him was chaos. Social intercourse, that complicated network of questions and answers, of what one can and can't do, of play, and of getting out of tight spots, also continued to be a nightmare for him. This explained his extreme dependence; he needed help with everything. Because of this he found it very hard to keep busy. Away from school, the void was even greater. The school holidays were an endless attempt to kill time.

John's language also developed slowly. He remained confused about the use of personal pronouns. He often repeated what was said to him, seldom answered questions, frequently confused the meanings of words or took words at face value. His lack of imagination was particularly striking. He had no ideas of his own because he couldn't formulate them. He simply copied what other people said.

His odd behaviour continued: the repetitive actions, rituals around eating and sleeping, his attachment to all sorts of objects, his outbursts of terrified crying and his unpredictable tantrums. During primary school, John remained a difficult child, a heavy burden on his parents and teachers and someone incomprehensible to his classmates. To them he was a strange figure, sometimes he even frightened them. Mostly though he was a figure of fun, a laugh, if only because he believed everything, you could tell him anything and he thought it was true, he took it all literally. He was the ideal person on whom to work off aggression, the perfect scapegoat.

It would be endless listing all the punches, kicks, bruisings, torn clothes, lost schoolbags, gloves and so on he put up with. It would be equally impossible to enumerate all the punishments, scoldings and blows he received from teachers over the years. The lack of understanding at schools is vast. But so is good will. The vast store of human energy expended by his parents, after school, at week-ends and holidays, is indescribable. When John sat at his desk with his homework, his mother sat next to him, steady as a rock. Explaining words, repeating the lessons, posing questions designed to help him. When John was uncontrollable and his parents had to put up with outbursts of screaming and tantrums they must have often felt at the end of their tether.

Here is his report at the end of primary school:

'John has learned to read and write and above all, to do maths. He can go on to secondary school. But John is a very strange boy who often talks to himself and only rarely to anybody else. A boy who does not understand the world and moreover is not understood by it, one who has no friends but doesn't seem to mind as he doesn't realize it. A boy who always stays at home with his parents and is bored there because he can't entertain himself. John stands out from others of his age group because of his naivety: he is unable to judge if things which happen are good or bad, safe or dangerous. The age gap grows.'

By now it must be becoming apparent that where a child with autism will do best, be it a homogeneous or heterogeneous environment, segregated or integrated, must be determined on the basis of individual assessments. There are no instant remedies. But the essential question is this: can the student or the adult adapt sufficiently to those people around him who understand him?

People with autism are different according to the definitions of autism. They act differently in the classroom, in a living or work group; they have a different style of communication and social intercourse, a different style of imagination and a different style of activity. In order to help them, you must use different educational strategies. For example, there must be more thorough research on their uneven learning profile, more visual aids, more coherence in teamwork, more coordination between school and home, a specially adapted environment . . .

To develop these special educational strategies other means are necessary. The staff must be well trained. The autism approach is not based just on love, intuition and doing what seems right. Sometimes it is convenient to work in 'homogeneous' autism classes because:

1. Teachers who work only with children with autism are more sensitized to autism and after years of experience develop a 'feeling' for it.
2. Teachers who spend 60 per cent of their time with non-autistic children have more difficulty developing the specialized skills necessary. They do not think in sufficiently 'autism' terms to fully appreciate their 'otherness'. Moreover, it is normal for them to pay more attention to the needs of the non-autistic pupils who find it easier to ask for attention in the normal way and to interact with each other. Pupils with autism are more likely to be overlooked in such a group because of their behaviour.

In an article *The Journal of Autism*, Gary Mesibov sums up certain problems relating to the 'normalization theory':

1. There is too great a gap between what can be done in theory and practice. Principles often camouflage unsuitable practices. There is a great difference between the slogans of the normalization theory and reality.
2. The criteria are often vague and unobtainable.
3. The attention is often focused on administrative procedure rather than on the individual. Progress is registered by the number of hours in a class with normal children. The number of hours is not a sure sign of progress. Quantity appears to be more important than quality.
4. Differentiation and renewing are discouraged, since renewing is not necessarily 'normal'.
5. By paying an exaggerated amount of attention to the normal, the impression is given that we are dealing with an 'unwanted' 'that is' not normal group.

And above all, 'We need a theoretic system which accepts handicapped people and values them for what they are and not for what a small group wants them to be.'

In secondary school it was not necessary to choose John's subjects immediately. But here too, the initial period proved difficult: getting used to all the new teachers, the number of students, the constant change of classrooms. The teachers had deep reservations about John's autism. Most of them had never even heard of it. The parents insisted on explaining his situation. In particular, they described John's behaviour and the staff was told how to respond to it. Most of the teachers reacted sceptically at first. The form teacher would have the primary responsibility for John. They mentioned the term 'special education'. Still John had at least to try to get along in this school. It was explained to his fellow students that he would often need help, finding his books, finding the right page, finding the right classroom. The students were also told that John might sometimes react strangely. The students were understanding. At school John passed the first year and got a technical qualification in woodwork.

In the second year he took the course in furniture making. He had to repeat the third year, he failed his general studies. And that was the end of John's secondary education.

He did get his certificate in the end. What happened to John in the next seven years as he grew up to reach adulthood is another long story. I'll try to keep it short.

First, his language problems proved a major obstacle for a standard education. The symbolism and metaphors were incomprehensible to him. Expressions such as 'he lost face' or 'he didn't have a leg to stand on' had him searching for legless, faceless people. If the teacher said 'Excellent, John', complimented him on some good word, John would think he was angry with him. Abstract meanings like 'influence', 'social', 'economy', were difficult to understand and difficult to explain to him.

John also had problems with higher mathematics: the language was too complicated. Nevertheless, thousands of words and meanings were explained to him and clarified by his parents after school and this helped a lot. John's vocabulary grew considerably throughout secondary school.

Practical subjects went better. John was very interested in woodworking, but he didn't have enough time after school to practise it so from lack of time it never become a hobby. There was constant contact with the school. John's mother rang one teacher or the other almost daily, asking about the various subjects, how John was handled, the small daily problems. She became a much discussed character in the staffroom. A lot of teachers did their best to avoid her if they met her out shopping. Social adaption for John was a nightmare. First, he had difficulties listening as he couldn't follow a stream of thought. Because he was slow to understand, he often interrupted lessons, asking for more explanations. This irritated both the teachers and his classmates. John was the butt of teasing and intolerance throughout secondary school. Because he took comments at face value, he often misunderstood what was said. He would be sent to the wrong classroom, his satchels and coats were hidden, he was locked up in the lavatory, his bicycle tyres were punctured. He had virtually no contact with the other students and when he did – and he wanted it – it was usually disappointing. Everything that John said was 'stereotyped' and beside the point, it was always the same and bored his listeners. The few whom John called 'friends' were usually good-natured boys and girls who did not shun him and called him by his first name. John had few opportunities for human interaction. He wanted to be 'ordinary', but his awkwardness in getting along with others, his pedantic, schoolmasterly way of speaking, prevented him being readily accepted. He talked like a book and kept repeating himself. He never seemed to learn. At home a great deal of energy was expended teaching him how to carry on a conversation, how to answer questions. Every evening his father would tell him the story of 'tomorrow': What would happen at school, the order of his lessons. This helped John to go to school calmly. At least he knew what would be happening. Another important thing was John's growing realization that he was different. He felt his handicap. Beginning in the second year he would often come home with questions about himself. Why couldn't he do what the others did? There were a lot of 'why' questions about his language, his inability to talk as the others did, his awkwardness, the bullying. John was helpless and his parents agonised over how to explain things to him.

The didn't want to pin a label on him so they avoided the issue. But the realisation of his handicap also had a positive side for John. He wanted to be like the others and that led to conformity. Outwardly he learned to do what his classmates did. Now he is twenty and you wouldn't notice anything very strange about him. He has overcome that for good.

But his parents are exhausted. Throughout the years his mother has redigested all the lessons and adapted each one individually for John. If the hours were totalled up it would be the equivalent of a full-time teaching job. The neighbours helped from time to time, going over John's lessons with him in the evenings, especially when his mother fell ill from the stress with (mostly) psychosomatic illnesses and chronic exhaustion. Now there is the fear of the future. What about next year? Can John go out to work? He is still very dependent on his parents. And he is not competitive. Can he cope with a normal work routine? Will his communication problems lead to rejection? His parents realise that John will be staying with them now. They do not dare pose the next question: what about the future?

2.5. Valuing handicapped people for what they are instead of what a small group wants them to be.

Reread the last two sentences in John's story: 'His parents realise that John will be staying with them now. They do not dare pose the next question: what about the future?'

One of the most important considerations when choosing an 'integrated' or a 'segregated' setting must be: what will the children learn there? What they should learn are things that will prepare children with autism to face the future. Will their education and training be suitable? In the story of John, who serves as an example for many children with autism, it does not seem this was always so:

1. The development of communication skills was neither strong enough nor specific enough for an autistic child.
2. Social development was not included as part of the ordinary learning programme.
3. Self-help and domestic skills were not included in the school programme.
4. Specific free-time skills were not dealt with since most normal children develop these on their own during weekend and holidays.
5. Efforts were made in terms of work skills and work behaviour, but were they sufficiently future-directed? In the average integrated setting the question of which job the student should be prepared for is not raised early enough.
6. Many elements in the story give the impression that 'functional academic skills' were in fact not functional enough and had little potential for future practical application in daily life.

We haven't even mentioned the years of helplessness that John, his parents and his teachers experienced; could they have anticipated what autism would involve and what should have been done about it? Often the choice of an integrated setting results in a short-term victory, but the long-term needs are overlooked.

Kathy Quill studied the question of when integration worked and when it didn't. She believes that the whole discussion of integration becomes confused because attention is focused on the existing possibilities for placement. Inclusion of integration, she concluded, does not work if:

1. the student with autism is expected to adapt to the existing programmes and educational methods;
2. the behavioural problems of the student with autism are regarded as the focal point for integration;
3. no consideration is given to the unique learning style and unequal learning profile of the student with autism;
4. the programme is insufficiently intensive or coherent.

Inclusion of integration can only work if:

1. all professionals having contact with the student with autism have adequate training in autism;
2. methods and programmes are fully adapted to the student's needs;
3. the teaching staff form a real team and coordinate the approach;

4. the educational setting guarantees:
    a. practising what they learn in their daily lives;
    b. sufficient choice;
5. there is constant communication, especially with the family;
6. there is enough support for the family. The parents must make a
    definite choice for an integrated setting; it is not up to the profes-
    sional social workers to decide.

In an article on the same subject based on a number of opinion
polls and interviews with teachers, Richard Simpson and Brenda
Myles add:

1. The class size must be small (maximum 15–19 students per class
    that will be integrating one student with autism).
2. All teachers in an integrated setting must not only be well trained,
    but also have constant access to a team of specialists in autism.
3. Teachers must also be able to work with the consultancy team
    and look for solutions together. One-way traffic in which one
    party forces through his ideas does not work.
4. The teachers must be given extra preparation time. One hour per
    day per student with autism is the absolute minimum.
5. Voluntary help in the class is essential. This helps the teachers
    document progress, develop activities and learning plans, and
    generalize. The aides can work with the other pupils, leaving the
    teacher free to give more time to the student with autism.
6. Regular refresher courses are essential.

Moreover, if it is to be successful, a number of things should not
be overlooked:

1. The directors must have a positive attitude towards integration.
2. The positive attitude of the teachers regarding the integration of
    the handicapped student is the main factor determining its
    success.
3. The attitude of the parents of the non-handicapped students is
    also important.
4. The non-handicapped students must also benefit. They too must
    be sufficiently motivated and prepared.
5. The entire school community must be given adequate informa-
    tion about autism.
6. Students with autism must already have the necessary social skills
    to be able to concentrate in a group situation.

7. A coordination of both normal and special education is usually required.

2.6. 'Reversed integration' as the starting point

As you see, meaningful integration of students with autism in normal education is not easy but at least it moves beyond the naive discussion pitting 'good guys' who are in favour of integration against 'bad guys' who opt for segregation.

In every case the starting point must be a realistic understanding of autism and the future possibilities of the adult with autism. If we are to offer the best integrated environment for our fellow citizens with autism, more is demanded from society than is presently available. Students with autism have very little social intuition and their abilities are more likely to be overestimated than underestimated. Would it not be better then to start with an environment that offers them maximum protection? And to consider a more integrated environment as a possible 'final' goal of the educational process rather than a means in itself.

This brings us to the principle of 'reversed integration': the first step in integration must be taken by the strongest. The 'weak' student with autism is offered an environment and activities that are best suited to his abilities. Starting from this point attempts are made slowly to strengthen the weak, so that they can cope with us 'ordinary' people with our difficult way of communicating and behaving socially and our lack of consistency. This is not a plea for segregation but for tailor-made care, 'integration made to order', reversed integration.

The most suitable environment can be in a classroom for children with autism, for special needs students or for ordinary children. The choice (as if we had a choice this time . . .) depends on the individual and is based on the unique characteristics of each student and a realistic assessment made by the parents.

Let me give you an example.

A student with autism is sent to a normal class to play with ordinary children (with little preparation – this is an extreme example). Just think of all the new things that the child with autism has to cope with: the environment is new, the children, who don't know anything about autism, are new, activities are proposed which no doubt will be too difficult. In this case it is almost normal for the child with autism to be overwhelmed by all the changes and novelties and suffer behavioural problems. It is asking for it . . . But a first meeting with ordinary students can also take place more gradually with more careful planning, perhaps as described below. In an autism class in a normal educational setting, a few students are specially selected and allowed to play with children who live very difficult lives. They are told that these children are handicapped in a special way. They hear, see and feel differently from us. These children must be helped, but not everyone can do this. Each 'chosen' student is now told whom his partner will be at the end of the week.

Take Charley, for example. Charley can't talk with words, he talks with pictures. He doesn't know many games but he's good with puzzles. He still can't do them with anyone else so he'll be prepared throughout the week. And then you can do puzzles with him.

Meanwhile Charley's teacher has been busy. Charley can do puzzles by himself now but he's never tried it with someone else. He'll have to be prepared for this during the week. Each day the teacher tries to teach this concept 'visually'. What she is trying to teach is the idea of taking turns. She does this by taking a cube that looks like a dice. Whoever had the cube can take a piece of puzzle and put it in its place. Then the cube is passed on to the other player. Once the student with autism has learned to play with the teacher he can transfer this skill to someone his own age.

At the end of the week the moment for integration arrives. The pupil with autism now has only a small step to overcome. Everything familiar remains as constant as possible. He is in the familiar autism classroom, he is playing a game that he already knows, only this time he's playing it with a new partner. This is more than enough for a first step.

Carefully prepared the 'integration' attempt can be a source of enjoyment for Charley. And we must not forget that there are advantages for the ordinary pupil too. He feels the satisfaction of a successful effort. He will feel more capable and more motivated to play with the 'handicapped' autistic student again. (Unprepared attempts at integration can be disappointing for everyone, for the teacher, for the child with autism and for the ordinary child whose attempts to communicate and play have failed. Such failures only help strengthen the taboo around the handicapped.)

After that, students with autism who are ready can be sent to an ordinary classroom on an experimental basis for a few simple activities. The teacher in the ordinary classroom will be fully briefed on autism and can fall back on the greater expertise of the autism teachers.

The most important question, however, still remains: is everyone ready for this? Parents? Teachers? Above all, the student with autism himself?

Gary Mesibov's thoughts on normalization and integration are very valuable. He writes that until recently more effort was put into placing people with autism in the least limiting environment than into bringing them up and offering them learning experiences. Uniting these two will not automatically result in positive interactions. Hard work is needed. It is a valuable undertaking, a formidable challenge and it is not easy.

2.7. The emotional aspect

Below you can see the logo of our training centre (Fig 4.8). It is worth studying in detail. It represents the head of a mother, but it is broken into parts. At the very top you can see the head of a baby and under that its body. Mother and child do not form a complete unit; they are separated from each other in a way that is enigmatic, even puzzling. For those without autism the pieces of the puzzle only make sense when they form a whole (the relationship), but for people with autism that whole is less obtainable. Even within the whole, the separate pieces remain autonomous (a 'full' relationship is difficult). They understand less and are more caught up in perception. You can see the logo of the training centre as a symbol of both problems, 'meaning' and 'perception' (the whole and the details), and the tension which this brings, united in a single image: the child who experiences a fragmentary world and we who attempt to share the whole, the meaning of the world, with this child.

Figure 4.8: Training centre Logo

In this case it specifically concerns the meaning of the social relationship with the mother and the emotional atmosphere that goes with such a loving relationship, so close and at the same time so difficult to understand and therefore so difficult to experience. The logo directly expresses our concern about the development of a good emotional relationship. In spite of this some people wonder whether we neglect the 'emotional' relationship in our approach. Why is this?

This reminds me of a particular experience in France. When we gave our first lectures and training sessions there, some parents said, 'You must take into account the fact that it is different here in France. If you leave out the words '*amour*' and '*souffrance*' doubts will arise about the rest of the lecture.' At first we thought these parents were exaggerating. Surely even without using the words 'love' and 'suffering', it was clear from our entire attitude, from all our educational principles, that we loved the children and that we were trying hard to relieve their suffering. And yet, after every lecture we were questioned about '*l'amour*' and '*la souffrance*'. Bearing in mind the advice of those parents, we then always used the magic words in the first 5 minutes of future lectures, although we didn't otherwise change the content of out training sessions. And *voila!* What a difference they made! No more 'stupid' questions; everyone was satisfied. Why?

In France one of the main reasons is the training of the average French professional and the expectations they bring. Those who have associated autism for years with a lack of '*amour*' and too much '*souffrance*' will not drop this vocabulary overnight; they want to continue to hear these words. There is a similar phenomenon in a few other countries: in the usual training courses for social workers and educators, there is a lot of talk about the role of emotions in development. Thus these are words these professionals like to hear repeated.

Nevertheless, this is worth commenting on. The belief that cognitive impairments affect emotional development is a central idea in the development child psychiatry. Child psychiatrist Michael Rutter gave some striking examples in an article of cognitive impairment in babies with autism. Babies cry, for example, when they are given an injection by a nurse, but they do not appear to associate this act with him or her so they will happily let themselves be picked up later by the same nurse who just gave them the jab. By the end of their first year, this has changed. An understanding of pain becomes an important part of emotion during this period. Another example is bonding. Between 6 and 9 months of age babies are in the 'I want mother' phase – they have developed clear preferences. If they have to go to hospital during this period and are separated from their mother, they become acutely depressed and despairing. Yet earlier this is not the case. It is the result of cognitive changes. At first they are unable to retain a lasting concept of mother in their memory (just like that needle). The sadness is complicated even more as they cannot (yet) imagine that a mother who leaves will come back. Later they begin to understand this and can cope better with the situation.

> Speaking for me is still often difficult and occasionally impossible, although this has become easier over the years. I sometimes know in my head what the words are but they do not always come out. Sometimes when they do come out they are incorrect, a fact that I am only sometimes aware of and which is often pointed out by other people.
>
> One of the most frustrating things about autism is that it is very diffi- cult to explain how you are feeling: whether something hurts or fright- ens you or when you are feeling unwell and you cannot stick up for yourself. I take beta blockers sometimes to reduce the physical symp- toms of fear and although I can now tell people if something frightens me, I can never actually tell them while the event is occurring. Similarly on several occasions when I have been asked what my name is by a stranger, I cannot always remember it and yet when I am more relaxed I can remember phone numbers and formulae after just hearing them once. When I am very frightened by somebody or something or I am in pain, I can often make motor movements and a noise but the words just do not come out.
>
> Sometimes when I really need to speak and I just cannot, the frustration is terrible.
>
> *Therese Joliffe et al., 1992*

> If language is a means of communication, then language is also a means of expressing emotion. Nothing is less true as far as Thomas is concerned. One evening I found him crying in his bed (he must have been about five years old). I asked him what was the matter and he answered, 'Water, on his pillow' (he still had difficulty with personal pronouns and spoke of himself in the third person).
>
> 'But you're crying. Are you sad?'
> 'He is sad.'
> 'Why are you sad, why are you crying?'
> 'Water in his eyes, his pillow is wet.'
> Thomas can only express what he sees in words.
>
> *Hilde De Clercq*

A number of studies have shown that people have a more or less universal and inborn pattern of facial expressions, vocalizations and perhaps also gestures to express early emotion. This biologically determined repertoire is an important means for social coordina- tion. In this way people learn to tune in to each other; in this way the basic patterns of reciprocity are learned. What do we know about understanding the emotions of children with autism via early vocal- izations, gestures and facial expressions?

Derek Ricks compared the vocalization of a group of non-verbal children with autism between 3 and 5 years of age with those of control groups of normal and mentally retarded children with a development age of 8 months. The three groups were brought into situations that would trigger four different emotions: surprise, pleasure, frustration and demand. Ricks registered all the vocalizations on tape and played them to parents.

In the normal and mentally retarded groups all the parents could identify which vocalizations went with a certain situation, and they could do this for all the children without exception. Within the group of autistic children only the child's own parents could identify which vocalization belonged to which situation. They could not place the vocalizations of the other autistic children. This study seems to show that:

1. Children with autism lack this biologically determined repertoire. From the start their vocalizations are 'different' (just like their communication and their social interaction).
2. Parents succeed at recognizing their divergent vocalizations via a gigantic adaptation process. Through this they can 'decode' or puzzle out the vocalizations (not universal in form but unique to each person) of their own children. But the vocalizations of the other children with autism are different and therefore unrecognizable.

In another study the use and recognition of gestures was investigated (see Fig 2.2 p.21) Five groups of gesture were studied, but we will restrict ourselves here to the first three:

1. the 'deictic' gestures: probably an extension of reaching behaviour (present very early in normal development);
2. the 'instrumental' gestures: gestures used to organize the behaviour of others, such as 'come here', 'look there', 'go away' (present around the age of 2);
3. the 'expressive' gestures: to share feelings; for example a hand in front of the mouth means 'I am embarrassed' (present around 4 years).

The division of the sorts of gesture used most by the various groups was interesting:

1. With 'ordinary' children, 48 per cent used deictic gestures, 26 per cent instrumental gestures to influence the behaviour of others and 26 per cent expressive gestures to show emotion.

2. With mentally retarded children with Down syndrome, 25 per
   cent used deictic gestures, 25 per cent instrumental gestures to get
   someone to do what they wanted, and 50 per cent expressive
   gestures to show emotion.
3. With autistic children, 34 per cent used deictic gestures, 66 per
   cent instrumental gestures and not one used expressive
   gestures.

Children with autism then do not use gestures to communicate their
emotions. Once again, they do have feelings but it is hard for them to
express them, just as it is hard for them to recognize them in others (a
tear is something 'wet').

And facial expressions? In 1872 Darwin wrote that people have a
universal repertoire of facial expressions and that children have an
inborn ability to understand the meaning of these expressions.
Recent research with babies supports Darwin's nativist theory in
connection with the universal expression of certain feelings such as
sorrow, happiness, and anger. The recognition of certain feelings
through facial expressions also seems to be inborn, although this is
more difficult to prove.

> Looking at people's faces, particularly into their eyes, is one of the hardest
> things for me to do. When I did look at people I have nearly always had to
> make a conscious effort to do so and then I can usually only do it for a
> second. If I do look at people for longer periods of time, they usually claim
> that I seem to be just looking through them rather than actually at them, as
> if I am unaware that they are actually there. People do not appreciate how
> unbearably difficult it is for me to look at a person. It disturbs my quietness
> and is terribly frightening – though the fear decreases with increasing
> distance away from the person.
>
> *Therese Joliffe et al., 1992*

Much experimental research confirms what parents tell us and
what we find in practice: that looking at and interpreting faces does
not elicit the same response for autistic people as it does for 'ordinary'
people. For example, it is difficult for them to look at photographs of
people and classify them by feelings: happy and sad are clear for the
ordinary person, but autistic people will put faces into categories
according to whether or not they are, for example, wearing hats. 'Yes,'
said the test psychologist a bit desperately, 'but how does this photo
feel?' 'Soft', replies the autist, touching it once again.

Other studies show that people with autism have abnormal difficulty making sad or happy faces themselves. Ask them to make a

certain kind of face and the opposite expression may as easily appear:

> If I ask him to express his feelings – for example, 'laugh at mother' – the result is that he will curl up the two corners of his mouth for a fraction of a second, with no sign of laughter on the rest of his face.
>
> *Cis Schiltmans*

Children with autism can learn this just as they learn other things, but the recognition of others' feelings and their own remains very difficult. Once again how difficult it is for them to overcome the 'literal' and look behind the perceptions. Eyes in particular are difficult to read. Lovers are traditionally very good at recognizing the meaning of eyes ('What does she see in him?'), but what do eyes literally express? They move too much for autistic people, they change expression quickly and changes happen too fast:

> Thomas can't read facial expressions at all. He didn't use to be able to understand when an adult was cross with him, he often started to laugh when someone's face changed expression suddenly. Since then I've taught him the difference between 'happy' and 'frightened' and 'angry'. We practised with dozens of pictures and little Thomas can now name them all perfectly. But unfortunately for him we don't all have the same face and it is still difficult for him. When his sister Elisabeth looked at him crossly the other day, he asked quite seriously, 'Elisabeth, what are all those lines on your face for?'
>
> *Hilde De Clercq*

There are, of course, important consequences arising from the fact that babies with autism have difficulty with emotional understanding and emotional expression from the beginning. They do not appear to recognize the inborn 'signalling properties' of others and that in itself affects their ability to adapt to others. Strangely enough, ordinary babies seem to have a talent for recognizing 'abstract properties' (for example, 'humanity'), before they learn to read the details of their mother's faces. From the abstract they move on to details, the specific. It is different for people with autism: the concrete, the specific, interests them the most. That is why some researchers say that they suffer from birth from an 'abstract orientation disorder'. From the beginning they are oriented into the world in a different way, their position is anchored to the particular, they don't scan the world for likenesses and differences, they don't group their perceptions. This shortcoming obviously hinders their understanding and their ability to abstract.

Recent research shows that the physical movements of a baby are synchronous with the speech of his mother. This was established by a microanalysis of early social interactions. Researchers such as Condon, Trevarthen and Bateson indicate an inborn social tuning, a sort of preverbal 'proto-conversation', 'in turn' activities at a preverbal level. In short, there is an innate motivation to come into contact with the feelings, interests and intentions of others. Ordinary babies can 'share meaning' from a very early age, they can add meaning to perceptions and share them with others. There have been many academic discussions around this: should these skills be called cognitive or affective? Many subtle social and communicative skills are already present from an early age, inborn in the normal child, but not in the autistic. From the very beginning their 'social and emotional understanding' is disturbed, the possibility of distinguishing emotions, separating what is meaningful from what is accidental and thus developing cognitive planning. Cognitive plans are, incidentally, 'abstracted' from experience: we do not gain knowledge by duplicating each experience but by actively constructing something new each time, drawing on our previous experience. In autistic people we see many more 'echo effects', where they attempt to copy an experience exactly.

At around 3 months of age the ordinary baby's conversation-like exchange of communicative expressions is more obvious, and this is how the 'mutual extended look', so crucial for the development of bonding behaviour, slowly starts. Parents interpret this extended look as a sign of recognition. When it does not occur, it is experienced as a sign of rejection.

It is also important that this initiative comes from the baby itself: parents tend to wait for the baby's acceptance of 'eye dialogue'. This is important to the baby as well, because in this way he can control the social exchange. If he is not prepared for it and does not respond, the parents will not insist. That gives the baby a feeling of power and control over his environment. Babies with autism seldom or never take the initiative and as a result get less stimulation from their parents – certainly from the point that the parents begin to feel 'rejected'. No doubt they make hopeless efforts for a while to draw out some reaction from the child – unfortunately possibly with the opposite effect. Studies on the orientation response of autistic children show that they are quickly irritated by the processing of new and unpredictable stimuli, and these are found, of course, in changing social behaviour. Although parents no doubt react in a more predictable way than strangers, the predictability is not enough to offer the baby 'release' and 'comfort'. Ordinary babies learn quickly that people are predictable. The baby cries and the parents' look of concern brings release and comfort. This happens much later with babies with autism. Some do not even turn to people for comfort when they are older, they seek it from a favourite object. A lot of obsessive behaviour involving objects – for example, constantly playing with trains – can be seen as an attempt to fend off fear.

> But as a child, the 'people work' was often too stimulating to my senses. Ordinary days with a change in schedule or unexpected events threw me into a frenzy, but Thanksgiving or Christmas was even worse. At those times our home bulged with relatives. The clamour of many voices, the different smells – perfume, cigars, damp wool caps or gloves – people moving about at different speeds, going in different directions, the constant noise and confusion, the constant touching, was overwhelming. One very very overweight aunt, who was generous and caring, let me use her professional oil paints. I liked her. Still, when she hugged me, I was totally engulfed and I panicked. It was like being suffocated by a mountain of marshmallows. I withdrew because her abundant affection overwhelmed my nervous system.
>
> *Temple Grandin, 1992*

An illustration of this can be found in one of my own experiences during a training course. There was a nice bright 7-year-old boy on the course. He understood all the visual aids by the third day; he was a high-functioning pupil with autism. He took his transition card to his daily timetable, he took the word card and radiantly declared 'work'. The tasks were all on his level and he worked independently for minutes. The silhouettes explained what was expected of him. Could this bright child be autistic? There were some who doubted it. That is, until they talked to his parents. Then it appeared that the nice boy was a real tyrant at home. If he had too much free time he would begin to talk about lifts. He would go on for hours with no way to distract him. How strange: parents, home . . . The next day the students prepared a whole series of new exercises that were slightly less clear and less visual than the others. What happened? The nice boy immediately had his first behavioural crisis. Although he had always worked happily before, the first time he felt frustrated because of a lack of clarity, he began to ask how long the work would last. A moment later it started. He began to talk about lifts and couldn't be stopped . . .

Research shows that bonding behaviour is not completely lacking in children with autism. They turn to parents more than strangers, no doubt because parents are so much more predictable. Even such ritualized forms of being together form a bond, but things remain difficult and the bonding behaviour comes not only later but in a different way. Parents and babies are less likely to be in tune. The baby with autism lacks – because of his biological handicap – the development necessary for 'emotional response', for true bonding behaviour.

Because objects are more predictable, he normally learns more about objects than about people, but of course one does not build up mutual emotions with objects. As the baby with autism shares few emotions and experiences with others, he learns little about emotions and people.

The baby with autism does not learn much about shared feelings through imitation either. Imitation is important not only for the development of language and abstract thinking, but also for the understanding of emotions and social behaviour. On this subject Uzgiris said 'Copying something means not only recognizing the actions, but also the similarities between oneself and others'.

The earliest imitations come from mothers who imitate the behaviour of their babies and teach the babies to watch with interest. In this way they also begin to see how to take turns, and the child is given a glimpse of reciprocity and social togetherness. As we know, the development of imitation in children with autism is delayed and/or different so that here, too, the opportunities to learn empathy, about the feelings of others and, through this, about their own feelings are missed (knowledge of other people and self-knowledge come from our emotional relationships with others):

> Thomas didn't learn anything from copying other children: washing his hands, brushing his teeth, putting his coat on and off . . . I had to try to teach him all this step by step, his imitations always went very wrong. Strangely enough he always copied the noises and behaviour of other autistic children. This was often interpreted as attention-seeking or naughtiness. I kept asking myself if it wasn't instead divergent development in the area of imitation. Ordinary children in that situation would ask themselves what the hell they were doing among all these 'odd' types, or why they were making such strange noises.
>
> Ordinary children wouldn't have wanted to make themselves ridiculous by copying everything blindly. Thomas quite simply didn't understand the situation and didn't learn anything about the feelings of others; certainly he learned nothing about himself.

> *Hilde De Clercq*

By trying to understand the feelings of others, ordinary children also learn something about their own feelings. From birth babies with autism miss many chances to learn more about feelings.

However, before we come to the end of this chapter we must point out that there is a big difference between understanding feelings and having feelings.

People with autism can have very strong feelings; they can even be overcome by feelings that they themselves often do not understand. It was pointed out earlier that one has to have the point of view of a space traveller to be able to see and understand one's feelings with some perspective. We often say that we can almost see our lives as if they were films, but autistic people cannot do this, and, confronted daily with a kaleidoscopic reality, they find it extremely difficult to frame their feelings. Through this image we can better understand how they can be emotionally unstable, as their feelings are more often moved by details rather than larger events.

> Thomas is hyper-selective and oddly enough, he associates certain feelings with certain details. Once I was going to take him out. I had planned, explained and visualized everything down to the smallest detail. He seemed to have understood and looked happy and yet . . . Suddenly he asked, 'Will I go with the good mummy?' So I assured him that I would indeed wear my three-colour earrings. Then his happiness knew no bounds.
>
> *Hilde De Clercq*

People with autism can nevertheless be very sensitive to the emotional state of others, to the mood of a situation. But here too, the same thing applies: there is a difference between sensing the mood and really understanding it. There seems to be a part of the brain that controls our ability to sense mood, which is located in a different place from the part that understands feelings. People with autism do have feelings and moods but seem to find it difficult to cope with them.

Some professionals have a tendency to talk about emotional developments as if it were an independent unit that you can develop alone, apart from daily events. But feelings cannot be developed in a sort of fourth dimension, they do not exist in isolation, they are connected to objects, to situations, to people. This is why we often refer to the 'aboutness' of feelings. Feelings are about something, are connected to something, are caused by something:

> We looked for a number of activities which were associated with pleasurable moments. In the morning in bed, in the bath, at the swimming pool, dancing to music before bedtime. It was encouraging to see that eventually Brian seemed to get the message: hey, you can have a nice time with these

people ... After a while he even brought us the record to show us that it was time to dance. Doing things together began to mean something good to him. In the beginning it didn't make any difference if it was with mother, father or a stranger. But through experience he learned that it was always the same two who did certain things with him. We, his parents, formed what seemed to be a set pattern. Moreover we understood what he wanted if he brought us the record. You couldn't say this of everyone. In this way he slowly learned to experience us as 'safe'. We were predictable creatures, he felt all right with us.

Cis Schiltmans

If you put people with autism in places that as far as possible are adapted to their handicap, you maximize the chances that they will feel 'positive' (about themselves). If the situations are clear (there's no joy without clarity for someone with autism), if the tasks are adapted to their abilities and the materials are self-explanatory, you are on the way to developing positive feelings.

I find it extremely bizarre. Ordinary children love their parents. From this love for their parents they eventually go to school and learn to work there. When I look at my autistic sons it seems to be the other way around. They first learned to work and then from this they began to open more to the social world.

Elena Ahlstrom

If you put someone with autism in a situation that is too difficult for him, where the social expectations are too high, the style of communication is too abstract and the material requires more imagination than he is capable of, there is a good chance that he will feel 'negative'.

So saying, I do not claim to know everything about the emotional development of young people with autism nor to have the solution to every problem. There is still a great deal to learn; after all, their emotions are all very different. But we can at least try to understand that difference as well as we can. We must not under any circumstances make the mistake of assuming that people with autism need to copy what is good for us: we are too ordinary. Love is, of course, most important, but really to love someone you must try to enter his mind and help him with his needs and not project your own onto him:

I felt terribly tired that evening and instead of going through the entire timetable for the following day, I just said that after breakfast we would cook something together. We would make 'lasagne' and 'soup'. He asked which soup, I said I didn't know yet. That night he kept me awake. (I was so tired, so tired.) When he began to cry, intuitively I led him to the larder and

took the first tin of soup which came to hand. 'We'll make this soup tomorrow.' He smiled and took the tin with him to his room and put in on the
shelf. When I was leaving the room I heard him saying, 'Nice mummy'. I
heard it clearly. But did he know what he had said? I asked him why I was
'nice' and Thomas answered, 'because now I know which soup it will be. A
few minutes later he went calmly to sleep.

Hilde De Clercq

Sometimes professionals confuse the word 'love' with fussing,
emotional pushiness and attempts to keep them in a state of permanent dependence. In fact these are cruel approximations trying to pass
for love; in reality it is a kind of pity. Save us from that sort of love.

2.8. Social awareness and sexuality: an introduction

People with autism have sexual feelings just like everyone else but
they understand them less well. In many cases they will have a
greater need for protection against sexual relations that they do not
understand than for a permissiveness that is not connected to a realistic sense of responsibility.

In terms of social interaction people with autism behave 'differently', and in the light of possible sexual relations they are also different. For them having difficulties in going beyond perceptions creates
an important problem. Immediately, one can see how this can cause
problems with sexuality: sexual organs are, for them, no more taboo
than any other part of the body. How can such a literal-minded
person understand 'making love'? Understanding social reciprocity
in general already causes them problems. What can a sexual relationship with a long-term partner mean to someone who still has
problems simply understanding the intentions, emotions and ideas
of another?

In the following short introduction we will consider a few general
ideas on the sexuality of people with autism. These are a few ground
rules that institutions may find helpful. The information certainly
has to be individualized:

1. Anticipate possible problems before they occur and involve
   parents in the discussion. It is not a good idea to wait until you are
   faced with the first crisis.
2. The staff's attitude towards sexuality should be discussed with the
   parents: it is they who will have the greatest responsibility for
   imparting 'values' to their children.
3. Let the institution work out a clear philosophy on sexual values

with justifiable and unjustifiable interventions.

4. If the institution has a position on the sexual education of the mentally handicapped, remember that this must be different for people with autism (who have fewer communication and social skills).

5. Attitudes and intervention connected to sexual behaviour must be sufficiently individualized. For those who are sufficiently verbal, individual counselling with a trusted person is highly recommended.

In puberty, new behavioural problems raise their heads, just because this is a difficult time of change. In fact this is true for normal development as well. Yet teenagers with autism find it more difficult to understand and deal with the changes in their bodies. When will they stop? What else will change? Puberty often coincides with the first epileptic fits. There seems to be a neurological deterioration in a number of young people. During adolescence, just as their bodies need more activities, there are often fewer adequate educational programmes available and the possibilities for relaxation are fewer as well. When this happens masturbation can become, through lack of alternatives, a form of repetitive behaviour used to achieve relaxation.

The problems that arise around masturbation often occur because of insufficient clarity and not fully understanding where and when it is allowed, and where and when it isn't. Masturbation at an inappropriate time and place is partly a problem of time management. Young people with autism should learn that although masturbation is allowed, it is only appropriate at certain times and in certain places. Not, for example, in the workshop, during meals or in public. But it can be done in the bedroom. This is 'where' and 'when' information. For some of them you can develop a symbol (at picture or object level) for masturbation and integrate it into the daily schedule: 'No, not now. Yes, later. Look at your timetable.'

Most people with autism have not developed sufficient ideas of social norms to be ashamed or to be able to feel guilt. It is not a question of bad will, it is simply that at this level they are still 'innocent'. Feelings of guilt and shame are quite complicated and develop between the second and third year in normal children. However, in people with autism this is one of the low points in their uneven profile of skills. Therefore it is an absolute must for them to have clear rules about when and where masturbation is permissible and when it is not. The rules are best visualized (obviously such agreements work best in an educational environment in which other programmes and agreements are visualized. Sexual education that is isolated from other forms of education will not work.)

Young people who have adequate verbal skills may perhaps be less nervous if they are given some lessons on parts of the body: what they are for and what the differences are between the male and female body (including the sexual parts, and with the same factual explanation as for the other bodily parts. The taboo is ours, not theirs.) The advantages and disadvantages of this sort of sexual education must be individually weighed.

Before we continue to talk about a sexual relationship, a word about 'echo behaviour' or 'echo- praxia'. If the same individual cognitive style is at the basis of certain problems in communication, imagination and social behaviour, it is logical to think we will find an echo effect in actions as well as in words. There, too, an inflexible association often replaces flexible thinking. People with autism develop social understanding and behaviour with the means at their disposal, but they are not ours:

> Gerald comes home one evening. He has been to the autism class. It is winter and his father has a cold. Every time his father takes out his handkerchief to sneeze, Gerald panics and throws a tantrum. Fear, thinks his mother, but why? This is totally new behaviour. His mother knows that most behaviour has a concrete origin. What has happened to Gerald? Where did this new fear come from? Like a good detective, she has to find out. She starts her investigation and talks to all the people who have had contact with Gerald in the last few days.

And guess what? Two days earlier, Gerald had gone to the autism class but both his teacher and her assistant were ill. The head had asked someone not specialized in autism to take over, to look after the autism class. This teacher – and this is understandable – couldn't cope, she didn't know how to keep order. So she started to pinch the children's ears. Are you misbehaving? Well, look what happens to naughty boys.

Now we reach the key to the matter. This teacher also had a cold and she kept taking out her handkerchief all morning. Then she would pinch the children's ears. Poor Gerald hadn't understood anything about this difficult situation. Miss Brown gone and Miss Martin gone, the usual routines upset, singing songs instead of working. But he had seen something – a handkerchief and that ears were being pinched. Now Dad was also taking out his handkerchief...

Echo reasoning. Our goalkeeper who taught himself how to be a goalkeeper by watching TV also showed echo behaviour. Just like a gifted adult with autism who wanted to live by himself (in other words, not with his parents) and so looked for a hotel room: he knew that not sleeping at home meant staying in a hotel. He had done that before.

Even high-functioning people with autism show more echo behaviour than is realized. This is why I think that a different kind of thinking should be used when decisions are made in connection with encouragement or discouragement of a steady relationship. Don't naively 'normalize' straight away, first ask the question, should he be protected from naive moralization? Building up and keeping a steady relationship never follows set predictable rules.

Most high-functioning young people with autism, of course, want to have a boyfriend or girlfriend. Their classmates have them, it is part of being normal and they desperately want to disguise the fact that they are unusual. However, we must not encourage echo behaviour and end up achieving the opposite of what we meant to achieve with our well-intentioned help:

> She started a steady relationship with an autistic man. But I felt relieved when the relationship ended and she analysed the end for me. When I asked her why they weren't seeing each other any more, she said: 'We went to the library together, we had dinner together at Hardees and we went to the cinema together. Then we'd done everything there was to do together so now it is time to start another relationship.
>
> *Gary Mesibov*

I certainly don't mean to suggest that steady relationships between an adult with autism and an ordinary partner are not possible, but they are still exceptional. It is a positive sign for the future that high-functioning students with autism in good educational programmes can begin to develop a real feeling of togetherness. Moreover, their handicap often gives adults with autism a certain advantage: they are frequently too naive and straightforward to be unfaithful or to break agreements. This is one quality that is often greatly valued. Nevertheless you still see women who become a sort of nurse to their husbands with autism, arranging and planning everything as the man cannot cope with too many new things . . .

People with autism who are preparing for a steady relationship do, of course, need as much information on birth control and contraception as anyone else.

Chapter 5
The problem of imagination

Every evening we watch the news with growing disillusion: world events seem to be dominated more than ever by wars and disasters. Again we see children die of hunger in front of the camera. People are being executed yet again because of their political convictions. Surely this can't go on forever . . . We would like to do something to help, but everything we want to do seems so incredibly complicated, so difficult to organize, and eventually we don't do anything except look for a long-term partner, have children and take care of our family. Shouldn't we honestly admit that we all suffer from a lack of imagination, and from limited, repetitive, stereotyped behaviour and interests?

1. Theoretical understanding

1.1. Repetitive and stereotyped behaviour. Limited interest patterns. Qualitative impairments

Now I, too, am showing repetitive behaviour when I ask you once again to look at 'problems' through the eyes of people with autism, to enter their minds, to share their world in an attempt to help them.

Let us first read some comments from people with autism, think about what they say. After that we will together see how, behind so-called inexplicable acts, there is often an effort, a hidden attempt to communicate. Of course, one only finds what one looks for:

> As I walked back to my room, I thought about what the host had said and it dawned on me – me, 20-some years old – that I was different. In kindergarten I thought my classmates were different; in high school I sometimes felt alienated as if I didn't quite fit in, but tonight for the first time I realized that I was really different. I was autistic. I was a special individual.
>
> *Temple Grandin, 1992*

132

He had some kind of fixation with school-bus numbers. He knew all the numbers of all the buses that passed our house. He insisted that they be in a particular order. As soon as he got home from school he raced to the window to watch them go by, saying each number as it appeared. He was highly excited, giggling to himself. If however, the buses did not pass in the 'right' sequence, he fell apart – crying, yelling. He'd shout, 'Yes, it was bus number 3 – it was not bus 14!' It was clear to him that he needed to control the world around him, that his failure to do so tormented him.

Mrs Barron, 1992

I loved the sameness of all the buses – they were all the same colour and had the same words on them – but there were minute differences too, for instance, the number on each was different, and there were differences also in the shapes of the 'noses' (some very pointed, others rather blunted). My goal was to see all the buses the school owned in one year so I could compare all of them. I loved the way they looked when they were all parked in a line, and I got very angry when bus 24 was late and I had to go home before I saw it. It was not supposed to do that! It was supposed to be in that line with the other buses. I hated it because it behaved the worst and was often late.

One day I lined up my marbles at home just like the buses. I picked four colours to represent the four buses that came to my grade school. The blues ones were bus 24. Then I moved the marbles the way the buses were supposed to move – I moved the other three colours away from the blue ones. Next I put the blue ones where they had been – like bus 24 arriving late. I stared at them. I got so angry seeing the blue marbles by themselves like bus 24 that I threw them down the register. I started playing the game with cards. When the card representing bus 24 was 'late', I ripped it to pieces!'

Sean Barron, 1992

1.2. Creating order out of chaos, avoiding failure. People with autism trying to make sense of the world around them

In Chapter 3 we saw that echolalia (once thought of as a bizarre expression of language, one to be eliminated) can have meaning for someone with autism, that it can be a means of communication for someone who finds our language too difficult: he talks the way he is able to talk. Many stereotyped and limited forms of behaviour can be interpreted in a similar way. To put it in computer terms, if the input is lacking, the output cannot be completed.

In the same way that we explain certain tantrums and other behavioural problems as pre-communicative behaviour, we can see repetitive behaviour as a possible form of pre-symbolic behaviour. If someone does not understand the whole, his actions can have a fragmentary character. This insight, which shows us that people with autism understand the world in a different way (with a different cognitive style), helps us put some bizarre behaviour in context: it is their reaction to a life that is too complicated. Their inflexible way of thinking helps us to understand some of their 'illogical' fears.

Why is Steven so afraid to sit on 'green grass'? Even when his mother takes him in her arms and carries him across the lawn, he still throws a tantrum. Is it another autistic 'whim'? In Steven's case his mother knows that when he was 3 he was stung by a wasp in the grass. For onlookers, it didn't seem so bad. Steven screamed and the poison was sucked out. Only poor Steven didn't understand much of what happened. He simply felt an intense horrible pain and didn't know why. All he knew was that he had been sitting on green grass. He thus associated the pain with a perceptual detail because he did not understand the real reason for it. It had stayed in his memory: grass means danger, green means pain. Now he worries even if his mother dresses him in a green jumper.

You can see in this a similarity to certain echolalia utterances. First, one detail takes precedence over the whole; second, the original 'learning situation' takes on a permanent character. We can add many examples to this one: why must one boy's glass always be filled two centimetres high? Why must every chair in the house be put in a certain place and not be moved? In the film *Rain Man*, why did Rain Man insist that the maple syrup was on the table before the pancakes and not after? Why was Monday always spaghetti day? Why did his bed have to be put under a window and his shoes placed in front of the bed? Why did the book always have to be put in exactly the same place on the bookshelf?

Those who have no other anchors in understanding look for anchors in perceptions. It makes sense to assume that through a lack of understanding, many people with autism learn the world 'by heart' and that a continuous rediscovery of a predictable world gives them a sense of security: order remains. Seen through their eyes, much of the bizarre behaviour is not so crazy. If the order in our world is too difficult to comprehend, they will create their own order. In their own way, they are perfectionists: in their world things must be right.

High-functioning young people with autism were asked to make lists of things they liked and disliked doing as children. In one list of dislikes one boy had put 'doing puzzles'. That clashes with the cliché about autism interests. So someone asked him why he did not like doing puzzles. The answer was illuminating: because a piece had got lost. Things had to be right. If order is disturbed, they have difficulties. But as people with autism do not have much understanding of the creation of order, we will have to create a (perceptual) order that they can 'see'.

In one particular family there were no doors in the house any more because 'Our son can't cope with them.' If he threw a ball, his father ran after it to bring it back because otherwise 'Our son has a tantrum.' Their dear son had definite criteria for a 'meaningful' life, and the whole family had become a victim of it.

1.3. Development of the imagination in ordinary children and in children with autism (Table 5.1)

Table 5.1:

Age in months

	Normal development	Development with autism
6	Undifferentiated actions on one object at a time	
8	Actions differentiated in terms of characteristics of objects. Use of two objects in combination (not socially appropriate use)	Repetitive motor movements may dominate waking activity
12	Socially appropriate actions on objects (functional use of objects) Two or more objects related appropriately	
18	Frequent symbolic acts (pretends to drink, to talk on the toy telephone, etc.)	
24	Applies pretend play routines to dolls, stuffed animals, adults (e.g. 'feeds' doll) frequently Pretend actions not limited to own routine (e.g. pretends to iron) Sequence of pretend actions develop (feeds doll, rocks and puts it to bed) Pretend play triggered by available objects	Little curiosity/exploration of environment Unusual use of toys – spins, flips, lines up objects
36	Symbolic play preplanned – announces intention and searches for needed objects Substitutes one object for another (e.g. block for car)	Mouthing of objects often persists No symbolic play Continuation of repetitive motor movements – rocking, spinning, toe-walking, etc.

Table 5.1: contd

Age in months

	Normal development	*Development with autism*
	Objects treated as agents capable of independent activity (e.g. doll is made to pick up own cup)	Visual fascination with objects – stares at light, etc. Many show relative strength in visual/motor manipulations, such as puzzles
48	Sociodramatic play–pretend play with two or more children Use of pantomime to represent needed object (e.g. pretends to pour from absent teapot) Real-life and fantasy themes can sustain role for extended period	Functional use of objects Few acts directed to dolls or others; most involve child as agent Symbolic play, if present, limited to simple, repetitive schemes As more sophisticated play skills develop, still spends large amounts of time in less sophisticated activity Many do not combine toys in play
60	Language is important in establishing theme, negotiating roles and playing out drama	Unable to pantomime No sociodramatic play

From Watson, L. and Marcus, L. Diagnosis and assessment of preschool children. In Schopler, E. and Mesibov, G (eds) *Diagnosis and assessment in autism*, London, Plenum Press, 1988.

1.4. Beyond perceptions. Details or the whole? The puzzle of the puzzle

In her book *Autism: explaining the enigma,* Uta Frith speaks of the 'constant search for coherence.' People with autism are less 'caught up in the meaning' and more interested in details. The spontaneous orientation towards a meaningful whole hinders them less than us in finding answers. It is from this that the expression 'the puzzle of the puzzle of autism' comes. The word 'puzzle' comes from 'puzzling', i.e. fascinating or bizarre. The fascination lies in the fact that separate pieces of a puzzle do not mean much in themselves: they only take on meaning when the puzzle is finished and the separate pieces cease to exist. For someone with autism this is often not the case. The details are more valuable and they continue to be valuable when the puzzle is finished. The whole does not appear to be as interesting – puzzles are even made upside down and when they are finished they are often not looked at.

People with autism are puzzling.

Look at the next two drawings (Figure 5.1) one of a shape board, the other of a hand puppet.

Both objects in Figure 5.1 are associated with play and free time activities. As we know people with autism are talented with one of these objects, but rather weak with the one. Have you ever tried to understand why? I think that we can explain the strengths and weaknesses from their different cognitive style and their difficulty in being 'creative' and to add meaning to their perceptions and to go beyond literalness. The difference between the form board and the hand puppet strongly correspond to the difference between instrumental and expressive gestures in the chapter on communication. In order to be able to solve the formboard one does not need to add much meaning perception. The material speaks for itself. Just looking says it all: triangle in triangle, square in square, circle in circle. As soon as someone with autism has reached a certain developmental age, they

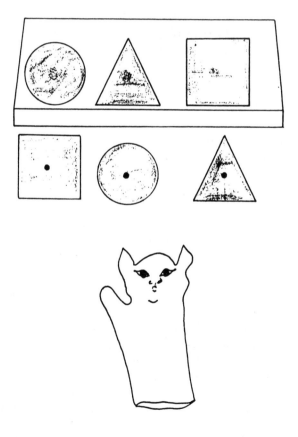

Figure 5.1: Shape board and hand puppet

will not have any difficulty in completing the formboard. Often it is the contrary: he has a peak skill, higher than his general developmental age. With the hand puppet the story is different: a hand puppet 'does not speak for itself'. The person with autism will look for minutes at the line (mouth) and the circle (eyes). Pure perception does not tell him what could be done with a puppet. With this toy one has to be creative and inventive and needs to have imagination, one needs to go beyond perception.

1.5. Stereotyped body movements. An obsession with the parts of objects. Unusual sensory reactions

Much repetitive or limited behaviour and interest can be associated with a low level of development in general and is therefore not exclusively 'autistic'. Nevertheless, in this and the following paragraphs, using quotations from high-functioning individuals with autism, I will try to understand how they see some of these unusual behaviours themselves. Although some of this behaviour seems very bizarre to us, we can help them better when we understand that it does have a purpose to them: 'The first step in helping someone else is to see things through his mind.' I have consciously avoided making many comments; the examples speak for themselves.

People with autism have bizarre reactions (they react too strongly or too little) to visual, auditory and tactile stimuli:

> My hearing is like having a hearing aid with the volume control stuck on 'super loud'. It is like an open microphone that picks up everything. I have two choices: turn the mike on and get deluged with sound, or shut it off. Mother reported that sometimes I acted like I was deaf. Hearing tests indicated that my hearing was normal. I can't modulate incoming auditory information. Many autistics have problems with modulating sensory input.
>
> *Temple Grandin, 1992*

> Throughout my life, I have had as much difficulty in trying to understand sounds as I have had in trying to understand words. I have come to this conclusion quite recently, as I am still frightened of so many sounds that I cannot obviously be interpreting them correctly. The following are just some of the noises that still upset me enough to cover up my ears to avoid them: shouting, noisy crowded places, polystyrene being touched, balloons being touched, noisy cars, trains, motorbikes, lorries and aeroplanes, noisy vehicles on building sites, hammering and banging, electric tools being used, the sound of the sea, the sound of felt-tip or marker pens being used to colour in, and fireworks. Despite this I can read music and play it and there

are certain types of music I love. In fact when I am feeling angry and despairing of everything, music is the only way of making me feel calmer inside.

Therese Joliffe et al., 1992

In my total horror of sounds, the sound of metal was an exception. I really like it. Unfortunately for my mother, the doorbell fell within this category and I spent my time obsessively ringing it.

Donna Williams

Many high-functioning individuals with autism – and this should not surprise us – also talk of their pleasure in certain visual stimuli. 'I love looking at lights, at gleaming metal and everything that sparkles.' Donna Williams speaks of a hypnotic fascination with dust particles in light. She also liked blinking her eyes or putting the light on and off quickly to get the same effect as a strobelight.

If I twist my fingers in my eyes, I won't go mad.

I am 35 years old and I'm autistic. I jump up and down on the spot a lot and flap my arms about. I am so autistic that I don't have to pay taxes . . . Life is a constant burden.

David

Temple Grandin talks about her ambivalent attitude to physical contact. On the one hand she longs for it; on the other she is afraid: when being hugged people are too overwhelming for her.

I always feel that I can understand things better through my fingers. Two of my relatives, one of whom is a clinical psychologist and the other a psychiatrist, both say that it appears that I am trying to compensate for my lack of auditory, and particularly my lack of visual, understanding by making use of my fingers, sometimes, they said, just as though I was blind. My consultant psychiatrist said something like this as well because I was always pulling him and touching him in a way that he said his other patients would not have dared to. He said that most people would not realize that I was in fact actually communicating with him, even if it was in an unorthodox way.

On the other hand I tend not to like kisses, hugs and cuddles very much. If I do give anybody a hug and cuddle it has to be when I feel like it, not when they want it. The only person who gets a hug at the moment is my consultant psychiatrist. My GP says he is a very lucky man but I do not understand what luck has got to do with a hug. I usually find what other people call jokes very difficult to understand, so I rarely laugh at them. I do laugh occasionally but it is rarely because I have found anything particularly funny, rather it is a repetition of the sound of somebody else laughing. It is interesting to try it out and makes you feel safer if you had heard this sound at a time when you actually felt a bit safer than you do at this moment. Similarly what other people call odd hand movements and what people refer to as grimaces are not meant to be annoying. They, too, give a sense of control, safety and perhaps pleasure.

Therese Joliffe et al., 1992

I had a big problem with food. I liked to eat things that were bland and uncomplicated. My favourite foods were cereal – dry, with no milk – bread, pancakes, macaroni and spaghetti, potatoes, and milk. Because these were the foods I ate early in life, I found them comforting and soothing. I didn't want to try anything new.

I was supersensitive to the texture of food, and I had to touch everything with my fingers to see how it felt before I could put it in my mouth. I really hated it when food had things mixed with it, like noodles with vegetables or bread with fillings to make sandwiches. I could NEVER, NEVER put any of it into my mouth. I knew if I did I would get violently sick.

Once when I was very small, I tried to eat a banana for my grandmother, but I couldn't do it. So from then on I refused to eat any of the other fruits. I wanted to eat the things I was used to; the others were threatening to me. When Mom tried to get me to eat something new I got very angry with her – I KNEW what I wanted!

Sean Barron, 1992

Temple Grandin wrote that she couldn't stand the texture of certain clothes. On Sundays she had to wear clothes to church which were different from the ones she wore during the week:

I often misbehaved in church, because the petticoats itched and scratched. Sunday clothes felt different from everyday clothes. Most people adapt to the feeling of different types of clothing in a few minutes. Even now, I avoid wearing new types of underwear.

It takes me three to four days to fully adapt to new ones. As a child in church, skirts and stockings drove me crazy. My legs hurt during the cold winter when I wore a skirt. The problem was the change from pants all week to a skirt on Sunday. If I had worn skirts all the time, I would not have been able to tolerate pants. Today I buy clothes that feel similar. My parents had no idea why I behaved so badly. A few simple changes in clothes would have improved my behaviour.

Temple Grandin, 1992

Up to the age of seven or eight I spent hours enjoying running my fingers over and scratching on the edge of my pillow case which had embroidery around it. I still do this now with different surfaces, especially if it feels good and makes a small sound, although I am frightened of some things, like polystyrene. I am frightened of its feel and the sound of it being touched.

Therese Joliffe et al., 1992

I remember lying on the floor picking at the carpet with my fingers. It's one of the first things I do remember. The feel of some thing that was not perfectly smooth was wrong to me – I picked at anything that did not have a solid surface. One rug in our house had many small ridges; by scratching them I could tell that all of the rug was the same, even if it looked different. I had to keep picking at it to be sure that the whole rug was the same, all of it. It must not change!

When I was a little older, I felt terrible walking around the house in my bare feet. It felt strange and awful to stand up and be still when I had no shoes on. My feet were extremely sensitive. So, when I had to be barefoot, I tucked my toes underneath so I could pick at the carpet with them. No matter how many times I touched the rugs, I kept on doing it to reinforce my feeling of security and to reassure myself that the rugs were the same each time.

Sean Barron, 1992

One of my favourite things was chains; I loved the texture of chains. Each link looked the same and even felt the same as all the others. Because chains on our garage were too high for me to reach, they were very mysterious to me – I wanted so much to touch them, but I had to use a stick instead. Since I couldn't reach them with my hands, I made them swing. I really loved the repetition of the swinging movements – I wanted to see the chains from all different heights and angles. The more I saw them swing, the more entranced I became, and the more I wanted to do nothing but watch them. It was what I loved. It was my routine. My mother kept trying to interrupt me, but that never stopped me.

Sean Barron, 1992

I also liked collecting the lids of tubes of Smarties. These were orange, green, blue, red and yellow and had a letter of the alphabet on. I had more orange ones and only a few blue ones and I never got all the letters of the alphabet. The only problem was that I wanted to take the lids off all the tubes of Smarties when I was in a sweet shop so that I could see what the letter was underneath and this seemed to make people angry.

Therese Joliffe et al., 1992

I really loved to look into car windows at the speedometer; my real interest was the needle. I tried to see as much of the needle as I could – this gave me a strong feeling of joy.

One day I went out into the road. In the back of my mind I sensed that a car was coming, but it didn't mean danger to me. My obsession was too strong and I felt invincible. I had to see the speedometer! The man driving the car stopped, grabbed hold of me, and took me to the house. I couldn't imagine what I had done – why was he so angry with me when all I wanted was to look inside his car? He scared me. Then Mom got furious with me, and once again I knew that just because I liked looking at speedometers, I was going to be punished. It was clear to me that whatever I loved doing was wrong – especially in this case, when a perfect stranger got angry with me as well. I couldn't figure out why looking in somebody's car was so terrible.

Sean Barron, 1992

1.6. Unusual reactions of discomfort to changes in the environment. Exaggerated insistence on set routines. Unusual lack of interests and obsessions within a small range of interests.

I loved repetition. Every time I turned on a light I knew what would happen. When I flipped a switch, the light went on. It gave me a wonderful feeling of security because it was exactly the same each time. Sometimes there were two switches on one plate, and I like these even better; I really liked wondering which light would go on from each switch. Even when I knew, it was thrilling to do it over and over. It was always the same.

People bothered me. I didn't know what they were for or what they would do to me. They were not always the same and I had no security with them at all. Even a person who was always nice to me might be different sometimes.

Sean Barron, 1992

I like opening and closing the doors of some of my toy cars, and in particular watching the wheels as I turned them round. I used to put them one behind the other in a long line so that it looked like there was a long traffic jam, although this was not the intention: I used to put Lego bricks into long lines as well.

I had hundreds of plastic toy soldiers. I put them in a big glass jar and I used to like quickly turning the jar and looking at the different colours and patterns.

Therese Joliffe et al., 1992

Martin's mother on his compulsiveness:

Like all autistic people Martin had compulsive interests. His were the wheel, drains and holes, the moon, numbers such as birthdates and people's ages; travel, particularly to the Mediterranean.

Also: getting a tan quickly – he would even cover himself with shoe polish, smoking cigarettes to look tough and trying to be like the other boys by speaking with a special accent. Sooner or later he got over them all.

On the subject of his compulsive thoughts, 'Martin's problems',
Martin himself listed them:

1. The big, but mostly the small, shock problem (author's note: Martin
    would stick his fingers in electric plugs to measure the voltage)
2. What granddad does when I touch the television too much without
    asking

What happens if:

3. I push Mark into a dirty canal or the river
4. I laugh at someone or scold them
5. I break something by accident or on purpose
6. I frighten someone on purpose
7. I tickle someone
8. I push a boy into the water
9. I break someone's arm on purpose or by accident
10. I am in a hurry to eat in the dinner queue
11. I throw boiling water on someone
12. I push someone in the queue
13. I hit someone on purpose for no reason
14. I hit someone for a reason
15. I take something from another boy without asking
16. I throw a bucket of water over someone
17. I take someone's trousers off
18. I put suntan lotion on someone who doesn't want it
19. Korea drops atom bombs
20. I kill someone by accident
21. I touch someone by accident

There were some identical doors in the room. I had to and would find out
what was behind them: was there a dead end or did they open into other
spaces? I felt better when I saw the doors. Before I saw them I felt uneasy
because my routine was broken by coming to this room. As soon as I started
opening and shutting the doors, I felt a lot better.

Of course I had to keep doing it even when I knew what was behind
every door – you never knew if something had changed in the meantime . . .
I had to look behind all the doors, without doing it, I couldn't be sure.

And also:

I developed my own defences. One of these was pretending to be a bus.
Like each of the buses parked outside the school, I had my own route. The
hallways were my roads, and I worked out my route and followed it
precisely every single day. I needed to feel in control; I despised my school
bus for consistently being one of the first to arrive, for controlling me, so I
adopted a route through the halls that meant I'd be the last person to get
wherever I was going.

This method helped counteract my anger and helplessness – feelings I

always got when I looked outside and saw my bus already sitting there ten
minutes before dismissal!

Sean Barron, 1992

K. knows everything about all the local authorities in Yorkshire. He thinks it is strange that Peter, who is the coordinator of
the home training service, knows much less about them than he
does: 'I don't understand how someone with a university degree
like you doesn't know everything about Yorkshire local authorities.'

I went to Chapel Hill, to a group home for high-functioning
adults. Michael had a passion for geography. He was well prepared
for the visit of a Belgian. He asked me about the height of the
Baraque Fraiture and Antwerp Cathedral. He found it very odd that
I knew so little about heights. Later he also told me that he knew that
people in Belgium speak different languages: 'The high-functioning
Belgians speak French, the low-functioning ones speak Dutch.'

I went to visit Demetrious Haracopos in Denmark. We went to
visit the Museum of Modern Art. A group of better-functioning
autists came in. Demetrious explained to me that one of them, Bent,
was mad about pigs. He knew everything about pigs, the breeds, the
feed used, their export and import figures. Bent saw Demetrious and
came towards him beaming: 'Demetrious, I am so happy! Do you
know what I have found out? That there are more pigs than people
living in Denmark. There are five million, four hundred thousand,
three hundred and twenty one pigs and only five million people.'

Dan's parents didn't understand what was going on. He didn't go
to 'school' any more the way he used to. He went to the 'classroom'.
If they used the word 'school' instead of 'classroom', he became bad-
tempered. Also, he wouldn't drink out of a beaker any more; now he
wanted a glass. And he wanted to go on holiday in France. He knew
everything about winemaking there and had marked the places he
wanted to visit on the map. All the villages ended in 'as': Vacqueyras,
Gigondas, etc. Later his parents found out that 17-year-old Dan was
in love with the school's 50-year-old cleaning woman. Her name was
Mrs Sas. Sas, Class, Glass, Gigondas . . .

I love following the weather forecasts and going to the library to gather
information on weather conditions throughout the world. I also collect all
the television programmes from all the American states to compare the
reception times with each other.

Gary Peterson

At this time in my life I found a new interest – astronomy. This science was titillating because it was the next best thing to a real escape – an exit from the jackass kids at my high school. Besides, just as with the TV call letters with which I was still fascinated, this was knowledge I perceive to be esoteric. Once again I established power. Astronomy filled part of my void of loneliness as well. I could deal with phenomena that were 'out there', and it helped me get away from my present situation.

I loved studying the various planets because that made it much easier to imagine being elsewhere. I basked in the soothing comfort of my own fantasies. Sometimes I would stare at photographs of Mars; then I would blast off and arrive on the planet itself, with its barren landscape and desolate craters. From Mars I could look down on Earth, so far away. Ohio was down there somewhere, but too far away to hurt me.'

Sean Barron, 1992

1.7. Nothing human is strange to me

Autism is 'different' but not that different. Analysing ourselves makes a lot of strange behaviour seem less bizarre that it did at first. Take 'repetitive behaviour'. Don't we like to repeat what we do well? And aren't both dancing and swaying pleasant repetitive behaviour? And 'limited' behaviour . . . 'Limited' is, after all, relative. Our pattern of interests is much wider than those of autistic people, but in the light of the choices possible, it too is fairly limited. In fact descriptions of behaviour such as 'repetitive' and 'limited' can also be applied to normal development.

We are also creatures of habit. We have our daily routines, our daily anchors. In periods of stress these help us to preserve our independence. We fall back on our habits, just like people with autism, in difficult periods. A lot of daily habits are difficult to change, and among the 'ordinary' population there are also many more people than you might think who have compulsive thoughts and rituals. Sometimes our habits and those of autistic people lose their flexibility. (An interesting aside: the 'tics' of normal people are treated with clomipramine, a strong antidepressant that works on the metabolism of the neurotransmitter serotonin, something which is also often unbalanced in people with autism.)

Suffering from 'compulsive thoughts' was once referred to as 'mental hiccups'. In a way you are the victim of an electrical 'ministorm' in the brain. Obviously, people with autism suffer more than ordinary people from 'doubts' and a need to verify that nothing has changed. This can give them the reassuring feeling that everything is OK, but in some cases they may become victims of a 'verification'

obsession. Then the involuntary primitive subcortical brain structure takes over. Instead of consciously choosing and wanting
thoughts, thoughts and actions come out in 'hiccups'.

To help someone we must first try to understand him, to enter his
mind. In this way we have discovered that echolalic expressions can
also be meaningful. We can ascertain that many repetitive and
limited patterns of behaviour are similarly not as crazy as we thought.
We have discovered some of the motives and reasonings behind them.
Without trying to give a comprehensive list, let us sum these up.

1. Doing things simply for pleasure

Examples are the word game with 'as', looking at the same colour
bus, liking the texture of material, enjoying patterns such as those
made by putting hundreds of plastic soldiers in a jar, putting things in
rows, etc. In an article about the life of his autistic brother, Robert
Fromberg rightly referred to the 'artist's eye': his brother had taught
him to enjoy visual patterns, many fascinating visual perceptions
that we never notice in ordinary life. Alongside this, bizarre motor
behaviour (flapping, spinning around, some kinds of self-mutilation)
can be a form of self-stimulation, which gives more satisfaction than
auditory and visual sensations, although this is difficult for ordinary
people to understand.

2. Carrying out an irresistible urge

'It is like quenching a thirst' is what someone with autism once said.
You answer commands hiccuped out by the subcortical structures.
Someone like Martin is afraid of this. 'What will happen if . . . I know
I don't want to do it, but what if . . .' Some motor tics first serve a
specific function and then afterwards become automatic.

3. Avoiding failure and defending yourself against the difficult and painful

'What I wanted was to be free. I thought up repetitive games by
myself. After all, I couldn't fail at things I had chosen for myself,'
Sean wrote. He developed his own route, just like the buses, as
compensation for the unpredictability of normal life. Temple
Grandin and others protected themselves against noise and other
stimuli that they found impossible to modulate: 'It was like a dentist's
drill.' This explains certain motor tics and forms of self-mutilation.
We bite our hands if a toothache becomes unbearable. You hurt
yourself to escape from a worse pain.

4. Learning more about the world in your own way

> If it is possible to teach autistic people by feel then I think this should be used. I could not learn properly how to put a knife and fork on the correct sides of the plate from just being told how to. But when somebody put the items into my hands and placed my hands down on the table in the correct positions, I learnt for good, once these steps were repeated a few times. Similarly, it was years before I could put my shoes on the correct feet until somebody took hold of my hands and ran my fingers along the sides of my feet and then the sides of my shoes. After doing this a few times, I began to put my footwear on my feet by running my hands along the sides of my feet and then my shoes to match up the correct ones.
>
> *Therese Joliffe et al., 1992*

This explains why people with autism want to touch things to verify what they see and hear.

Another way of learning more is to collect facts: learning air and train timetables by heart, or everything about Yorkshire's local authorities, the height of hills, mountains and cathedrals. Encyclopaedic knowledge does not demand a knowledge of flexible links. Facts are certain, ideas are often too flexible.

5. Reacting to stress

Falling back on rituals and habits can keep fear at bay and under control. Geraldine Dawson points out that the brainstem triggers a hyperselective mechanism if sensations become too complex. The more difficult a situation becomes, the more people with autism become hyperselective in their attention and fixate on details.

6. Giving way to the urge to explore, coupled with a low age of development

This point is associated with point 4 above (learning more). In normal development children often put objects in their mouths. They learn by tasting before sight becomes more dominant. People with autism often remain stuck at a particular age of development for much longer. If you then take into account that 'proximity senses' are of special interest, you can understand why they often keep objects in their mouths for an unusually long period, licking and tasting.

7. Maintaining predictability

This is associated with point 3 (avoiding failure). 'Everything has to be right.' This is the reason for the search for stability. The world of which children with autism understand so little has to stay as it was first perceived or understood at first. It must not change too much all at once. Even switching the lights on and off creates a simple form of predictability (while also being an experiment on the relationship between cause and effect).

8. Communicating through one's behaviour

Certain kinds of self-stimulation, including self-mutilation, express a need for a faster response from professionals. Parents also see that some kinds of physical restlessness means that the child is hungry or thirsty or wants to go to bed.

9. Escaping from a difficult situation

This function overlaps some previously mentioned functions. The 'flight to Mars' helps people forget the situation in Ohio, in the same way that we might use a film or a daydream. Certain rituals and repetitive behaviour of autistic people are avoidance mechanisms. For example, every time someone asks a difficult question, you kiss him.

Why are questions also always successful? Because the other person stops talking and drops his expectations of you for a while:

> I had a driving need to ask questions about the states because I felt I could not talk the way 'normal' people talked, nor could I take part in their conversations, since I didn't understand them. I had to compensate for what was lacking, and what better way than to show people that I knew all 50 states, their positions on the map, the shapes of each one? I needed to show everybody how smart I really was, and by asking the questions, I was doing just that. I never asked, 'What states have you been to?' but rather, 'Have you been to Montana?' so that I could show them I knew all the states.
>
> These questions were also a form of escape for me.
>
> *Sean Barron, 1992*

1.8. On play. Playful or stereotyped?

At one time professionals concentrated their attention on the language development of people with autism: if that got started the rest would follow. Or they read that the best prognosis was held out for young people with good social skills. If they managed to develop these, everything else would follow. We now know better than ever that people are best helped by developing their social and communicative skills but that their cognitive inflexibility limits the possibilities.

Belief in the magic effect of one particular treatment or therapy is sometimes called the 'Sleeping Beauty syndrome'. This has cropped up again in the last few years in some professional circles where unrealistic expectations of the effects of 'play therapy' are being maintained: if only that would take off. During the development of communication skills it is recognized that it is impossible to use a communication form with pictures if the child does not understand the connection between the pictures and the objects they depict. During the development of social interaction skills it is recognized that a child with autism cannot begin to share if he cannot even tolerate the proximity of strangers. But when it comes to the development of play people do not always seem to realize that, here too, evolution from the simple to the complex is gradual, moving in predictable steps. Ina van Berckelaer has pointed this out in numerous articles.

In the following overview I will limit myself to four major stages of play development. This information should help us to understand better certain stereotyped behaviour that occurs in the play of children with autism.

1.Simple manipulation

At the age of 4 months a child explores his environment through simple 'cause and effect' games. You shake a rattle and the result is always the same noise. An ordinary baby is also interested in other sensory effects: he sees how his mobile moves when he touches it, he strokes his teddy bear. He experiments with all the senses at the same time. There is considerable variety in his play.

This information will probably remind you of many older children with autism who are 'stuck' at this stage. Their play is simple and limited. They always repeat the same games, they push the train endlessly around and around, spinning wheels – repetitive, stereotyped, simple manipulations. Often they prefer proximal sensations: they will scratch a piece of material for hours at a time or lick an ashtray.

2.Combination play

Around the age of 8–9 months an ordinary child becomes a real detective. He sees and feels how things fit together. In the beginning the combinations are haphazard: a cup in a block is wobbly, a block in a cup is much better. Shapes fit in a shape board. Blocks can be balanced on each other.

Combination here means seeing the meaningful connections between objects. However, children with autism have their own idea of order and they are then at their best with combinations that are obvious: one shape fitting into another shape.

They do not really explore by using different materials in a different way. They are much more likely to repeat endlessly the same 'senseless' combination.

3. Functional play

During his second year an ordinary baby shows that he understands the purpose of objects. He takes a spoon or a comb and pretends to eat or comb his hair. Later he will start playing 'house' with miniature toys: he sets the table, pulls up the chairs. He still can't talk, but his play shows that he has ideas.

This form of play assumes that you can imitate and that is a difficult skill for children with autism: you must use another person as your reference point, understand that it is in your interest to copy him, and that he is an interesting model. The majority of young children with autism have not reached the level of imitation that would enable them to play functionally: for example, they would put the chairs and table in a row, or use them to build a tower. High-functioning children with autism do seem to acquire some functional play, but when we look further we see that this mainly consists of taking scenes from daily life 'literally' and always repeating them in the same way, with no variety.

The advantage of the first three stages, particularly for children with autism, is that the games have a visible result: if you combine, if you play functionally, you change the situation, you see the result of your action. The objects are always what they appear to be. That is not true of the next stage. Here we go beyond perceptions. This is more difficult!

4. Symbolic play

Functional play moves gradually into symbolic play. Something which does not exist is made to exist. It becomes a symbol of something else. Ordinary children do not have problems with 'pretend' games. They think it is fun to turn reality upside down, to distance themselves from it: to play mother and father, to be a bear or a train or to play 'school'.

Come along, come along, and join the magic circus of life. 'But people with autism have more than enough problems with one reality. Must there be another reality? In symbolic play the skills involved are those which go beyond perception, beyond the literal. For the majority of people with autism this causes difficulties throughout their lives. Take this moving example of a high-functioning boy with autism who tries to play a 'symbolic' game with his sister.

> Elizabeth was nine at the time and Thomas was nearly seven.
> 'Come on, Thomas, let's make a doll's house.'
> 'Yes, we'll make a doll's house.'
> Thomas goes to get his pillow and his blankets, not for the dolls but for himself. While his sister gets everything ready, he lies on the ground, his head on the pillow.
> 'Wait, let's see . . . The veranda will be our house.'
> 'Yes, our house.'
> 'And the cupboard can be the doll's bedroom.'
> 'Yes, the cupboard is the bedroom.'
> 'And we'll go and find some shoeboxes; they can sleep in them.'
> 'Will they sleep in those? They are for shoes!'
> 'Yes, but now they are dolls' beds.'
> 'Yes, the doll's beds!'
> 'The handkerchiefs can be our sheets, and the towels can be our blankets.'
> Thomas goes over to the kitchen drawer and pulls out a ladle. He brings it to his sister and says:
> 'And this, this ladle, that is . . . our ladle.'

Thomas's mother added this:

> At the moment he is still incapable of being creatively occupied. When I tell him stories they are all 'real life' adventures, for example, about a boy who makes pancakes with his mother – realistic, with no 'pretend'. If I use a 'book' to tell a story, he hardly listens but he notices every details: he sees that the water is 'bluer' on the first page than it is on the third page.

Adult Tom is still afraid when he sees depictions of Christ with a bleeding heart and a crown of thorns. At school there's a stuffed deer head on the wall. He always wants to look at the other side of the wall where the body should be. A nightmarish existence. Nightmares and dreams, yet 'another' reality . . .

> If parents complain that their children are bad at sleeping, it could be because the autism is affecting the child's dreams. If these dreams wake him up, it is very hard for him to realize that they are not real. It takes ages even with having a light put on afterwards to realize that what was experienced during sleep was just a dream.

Therese Joliffe et al., 1992

1.9. Free-time skills

When asking after a child in Japan, instead of saying 'How is . . .?' they say, 'How is he playing?' Play is so important to development. A child who plays well uses his imagination and understands the language and rules of game. If you compare the play of a child with autism with that of an ordinary child of the same age, you have to conclude that the play of the child with autism is not only backward but also 'different'. He communicates differently, experiences differently, plays differently. Autism is different.

When you recognize this, you immediately realize that there is no point in taking 'normal development' as the only point of reference for further development. Autism dictates another sort of progress. Eventually, it does not make much sense to continue comparing a child with autism with an ordinary child: ordinary children will always develop more rapidly. You begin to think more about autism development by itself: what progress has the child made since the last examination?

You also start to think about the future: what must be done to prepare the child for a meaningful adulthood? From this moment on, the approach becomes functionally rather than developmentally oriented. You begin to talk about 'free-time skills' instead of 'play'. You ask how the child will occupy himself in the abyss of time . . . To be able to occupy yourself is a very functional skill. In the future workplace there will be breaks, holidays and weekends. Even in the best of homes there is always time to kill.

'Free-time skills' is a typical 'autism expression'. Skills to fill time do not spontaneously appear in children with autism. They must be taught. Let's analyse the expression itself.

'Free' implies that you know (or see) the choices possible and that you are capable of making a choice. Free also implies that you have enough skills to recognize the choice and organize it. It means that you have learned how to bring variety into your 'free time repertoire'.

Then there is that word 'time'. Here you have the problem that time is not 'visible' that it is very abstract. Often you cannot see the beginning of an activity, you do not know how long it will last, and the end is also insufficiently visualized. How can you 'see' what you have to do after that?

How can we help people with autism with the problems of play, repetitive behaviour, stereotype behaviour and time skills? If autism is different, the approach to these problems will also have to be different.

2. From theoretical understanding to educational intervention

2.1 Do we work to eliminate stereotyped behaviour and behaviour problems?

We have to treat the causes rather than the symptoms. Autism problems are like the tip of an iceberg.

> Can you imagine that only a very few things give you pleasure and that all these have been forbidden? They claimed to help me by systematically robbing me of my personality.
>
> *Barbara Moran*

It should by now be clear that we are trying to treat causes rather than symptoms. We are often asked where we stand on behaviourism and conditioning. Without going into an academic discussion here is what we think.

In the first place it depends on what the questioner means by the words 'behaviourism' and 'conditioning'. In the most general sense, conditioning means rewarding desirable behaviour and punishing undesirable behaviour. In this sense all parents of ordinary children are 'behaviourists'. If their baby laughs, parents show how happy they are, and in this way they try to encourage the desired behaviour. If a child whines for ages because it does not get an ice cream, parents will make it clear that enough is enough: that behaviour is undesirable. By saying 'stop it' and frowning, we teach the child good manners. In the best sense of the word we are all behaviourists, even with children with autism. It is important that children learn what sort of behaviour is acceptable and what is not. It is, however, more difficult to show children with autism what is right and what is wrong in a way that they understand.

There are also what we might call 'strict behaviours', the symptomatologists, who do not bother much about the 'soul' of the child and ask few questions about the reasons for a child's behaviour. They want to encourage certain behaviour and eliminate others, including stereotyped behaviour.

Wait a minute! We have just made it clear, particularly through the examples of high-functioning people with autism, that much stereotyped behaviour has a clear function. People with autism want to create security and predictability, escape from difficult situations and protect themselves, ward off fear, stimulate themselves and receive rewards. Do we want to take all this away from them? And what price will we pay in human terms? Numerous stereotyped games obviously tally with a number of essential characteristics of people with autism. They conform to their inflexible cognitive style, they are predictable and they give them a feeling of euphoria. Moreover, they can be rewards and they don't need us for this. In other words they have a right to them. The traditional behavioural therapies are aimed at ordinary children and do not take into account the differences of children with autism.

Obviously, some stereotyped behaviour can hinder integration and be an obstacle to learning. But autism is in itself an obstacle to learning. Do we want to eliminate autism? If people with autism threaten to become the victims of certain stereotyped behaviour, of course they need our help. But in this case, too, the adaptation should work both ways. You can demand a reasonable effort from someone with autism, but it is up to us to take the bigger step.

In a questionnaire about behaviour problems at home sent to parents, problems with 'play' scored fairly high. For example, one parent said, 'My son can't entertain himself, he doesn't do anything with ordinary toys, he throws his brother's games around, breaks everything, won't play with other children.' What the parents saw was the tip of the iceberg. You can melt the tip down (through symptomatic treatment) but this will not solve anything in the long run. The bulk of the iceberg (autism) lies hidden under the water; it is there that the cause should be treated (van Bourgondien) (Figure 5.3)

Here are some possible causes for the behaviour of the little boy described above:

1. He has problems organizing his behaviour (he cannot see the beginning, duration or end); he has too few visual aids to take the steps needed in a game.
2. He uses material in a way which brings him more interesting results than those envisaged by the toy manufacturer for ordinary children.
3. He does not understand, for example, that dolls symbolize people.
4. He does not understand enough of normal life to invent games of 'normal life' with a doll.
5. He does not understand the language needed to play with ordinary children.
6. He does not understand the rules of the game of social play.

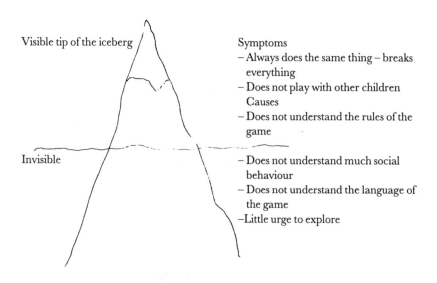

Visible tip of the iceberg

Symptoms
– Always does the same thing – breaks everything
– Does not play with other children
Causes
– Does not understand the rules of the game

Invisible

– Does not understand much social behaviour
– Does not understand the language of the game
–Little urge to explore

Figure 5.3: The iceberg – autism

Now you can see how the boy needs an educational approach in order to learn free-time skills, to amuse himself and to develop games. The use of visual aids will make him more independent. Specific training and education are the most important ways of treating behaviour problems and stereotyped behaviour.

One problem with treating stereotyped behaviours is that each is so different and can serve a variety of functions. Before we go into the approach to stereotyped behaviour in general, we will first look at and discuss the treatment of one individual case. Finally, we must conclude that even when we understand the whole picture of stereotyped behaviour, the treatment of it is always a matter of an individualized approach for each child.

2.2. An example: the treatment of John's repetitive and stereotyped behaviour

John's problem is that he puts his hand and all sorts of objects in his mouth, in a stereotyped and repetitive way.

John is a 7-year-old pupil. He is profoundly mentally handicapped, hyperactive and autistic. The fact that he puts his hand and objects in his mouth in a stereotyped way is a serious behavioural problem for his teachers. Because he has been in the autism class for

2 years and the problem still has not been solved, they want this particular case specially looked into. Are they doing the right thing?

It is important to know why he behaves likes this. In general I try to see the difficult behaviour of the child and our reaction to it as a form of communication. (It is counterproductive to speak of 'bad behaviour'. It is better to react by asking what causes this confusion.) So I put myself in the place of the child and ask, 'What is he trying to say?' because a lot of 'difficult' behaviour appears to be pre-communicative behaviour. Then, from my own viewpoint, I ask myself how I can explain to the child that, from his point of view, other behaviour can be more beneficial. We go to work in various stages (van Bourgondien).

1.An objective description of the behaviour

This is the first step: an objective description. It should not begin with preconceived ideas such as 'John is nervous' or 'John is impulsive'. It is important that professionals and parents see the behaviour with the same eyes. 'John is aggressive' can be interpreted in various ways. This does not help in getting a clear picture of the child.

In John's case, this isn't so difficult. 'He puts his hand deep into his mouth' and 'He puts objects in his mouth' (up till now, nobody has seen him swallow anything, but everyone is afraid this might happen).

2. What is the history of this behaviour?

First, if the behaviour started recently, we may perhaps discover that it was caused by a change in routine or some other environmental factor. It is then usually easier to change the environmental factor than it is to change the behaviour itself. However, if the behaviour has been present for years, it is usually wishful thinking to assume you can change it within a few days or weeks. The prognosis is more positive for recent behaviour.

When questioned, John's mother told us that this behaviour had really always been present.

3. Is a change in the behaviour really a priority?

That is an important control question. We have to see whether the objection to the behaviour is more than a question of personal dislike. Giving direct attention to one particular behavioural problem can take up a lot of time and energy. Is it really worth it? Maybe we should be focusing on other, more educationally important aspects. Moreover, what do the parents think? They must agree to a direct approach to behaviour problems. After all, he is their child; he is only with us temporarily. The most important decisions concerning the development of their child are, after all, their responsibility.

The teachers are astonished when John's mother says that changing this 'problem behaviour' is not a first priority. It might be in the long run, but at the moment it is not. Absolutely not. If John is stopped from putting things in his mouth all of a sudden, if things are constantly taken away from him . . . She is afraid that such an approach at school (a school that she finds very satisfactory) may prove too negative. John would not be able to cope with it.

She also gives the teachers an idea. At home she has been giving John a cloth to suck. She calls it a 'doo-doo', a name she got from a French friend. It is harmless and when John has his 'doo-doo' he is calm and does not look for other (more dangerous) objects to put in his mouth. Perhaps he could take the 'doo-doo' to school.

4. When where and with whom does the behaviour mainly take place?

This is another attempt to understand difficult behaviour from the point of view of the child himself: his 'why'. What is the function of this behaviour for him? If you observe it over a few weeks, taking notes, you may notice that the difficult behaviour occurs, for example, during recreation period, during work time or when he is waiting for the bus. Then you can begin asking relevant questions: does he have too much 'empty' free time? Are the exercises too difficult? Does he have to sit at the table too long? Is there a way for him to know how long he has to wait? You begin to understand that the questions are more about changing the environment than attacking the behaviour itself.

Some useful information comes to light about John. When I ask the question directly his teachers realize that John might behave like this in any situation, but he does so less when he is doing exercises at his work table. There, he is more interested in the work in his hands and is less interested in putting his hand or anything else in his mouth. He has something else to do. However, in his free time you see the behaviour more often. There he has to fall back on his own resources with no help from adults. In this situation the behaviour continues relentlessly.

5. What are the results of this behaviour for the child?

How do people react to it? Does the behaviour produce interesting results? And is the child trying to achieve these results through his behaviour because he has no other way to 'talk'?

You must know the ABCs of the behaviour alphabet before you react. A stands for 'antecedents': in what circumstances does the behaviour take place? B stands for 'behaviour': what kind of behaviour are we talking about? C stands for 'consequences': what are the (possibly interesting) consequences?

Sometimes we ask the parents to collect objective facts about the behavioural problems of their child, to note down when the child is difficult, in what circumstances and how the parents have reacted. A few weeks later many parents report that the behaviour problems are considerably reduced. The parents' behaviour – taking notes, creating some distance and not reacting immediately – has taken away the child's desire to seek attention in this way. The pleasure has gone out of it. The difficult behaviour no longer produced the desired response.

Another well-known and telling example is that of so many adults with autism who are in environments not adapted to their handicap, with endless free time; they are bored to death. They are unable to ask for attention in the normal ways – they cannot talk, nor do they have any non-verbal system of communication. However, they have discovered that they can get attention if they hit one of their fellow workers or if they bang their heads on the wall. The attention may be negative, but negative attention is better than nothing. In this way a behavioural problem becomes a form of communication: 'I'm bored. I want attention. Take some notice of me . . .' (Symptomatic treatment? Forget it. These people must develop free-time skills, learn to work, learn to communicate. Many behavioural problems solve themselves.)

In John's case neither his mother nor his teachers believed that John did it to get attention – he was not thought to be that calculating. And he did it when he was alone. They thought that it was more likely a form of self-stimulation.

6. How serious is the autism, and is the developmental level of the child high enough to cope with the situation where the problem behaviour occurs?

First, is the child settled in an environment where autism is understood and where the environment and programmes are sufficiently adapted to the needs of children with autism? If professionals are using a form of communication that is too difficult, if teaching methods are not visual enough, if there are endless periods of 'empty' time it is not surprising that there are behavioural problems.

In John's case such an evaluation had been made. The autism class was sufficiently specialized, the programmes individualized. But John is both severely autistic and mentally handicapped. Would it be possible to increase the number of work sessions (when he shows less stereotyped behaviour) and reduce his 'free-time' (when he shows more repetitive behaviour). This should not be a drastic change. John could not cope with that. Given his level of development, he should not be forced. Indeed, he has the 'right' to his stereotyped behaviour.

7. Now that we have enough facts to understand the behaviour, what do we do about it?

First, a generalization: it is always an open question whether intervention will work or not. Sometimes is it successful, sometimes it isn't. After all autism is so different. The important thing is not to be discouraged if it does not work.

In John's case the teachers were relieved by the analysis. John's mother was also pleased by the work done for her child. We were on the right path. Later on John would probably put his hand and other objects into his mouth less often, but first he would have to become more interested in other things. That was more difficult. During the discussions John's mother told the teachers about the 'doo-doo'. From then on John was allowed to bring it to school with him and use it during the free-time period. The teacher would consider the problem of the uneven division of work and free time. However, the discussion had shown her that she had been treating the stereotyped behaviour correctly through her treatment of John and through education without even realizing it.

In the end it reminded everyone of the Moliére play in which one character discovered he had been talking 'prose' all his life only at the point when he learned what the word meant.

2.3. Another cause, another treatment

The current principles of behaviour therapy would be different if Pavlov's dog had been autistic. If the stereotyped behaviour of people with autism often has a different function from that normally expected, perhaps we can discover different responses to it.

Here are a few mini-tips, easy to integrate into an educational programme.

1. Prevention: try to find out what factors trigger this behaviour and attempt to reduce or avoid them. The greater the understanding of autism, the easier it is to avoid problems.
2. Increase the success rate through proper treatment. The better (the more successful) the educational programme, the less need there is for stereotyped behaviour.
3. Stereotyped behaviour used as a reward. Want to play with the rope? Yes, you may, but first you must spend 2 minutes at the work table. Want to listen to music? Yes, but you may only do what you want if first you do what I want.
4. Predictability incorporated into the day's routine via individualized schedules.
5. Predictability in the duration of activities as explained by individualized schedules.
6. Individualized programmes for all the key skills: communication, free-time skills, work skills, work behaviour, social skills, self-help.
7. Visualizing sufficiently the tasks and work in an individualized way.
8. Sometimes a routine is broken just by changing the environment (the honeymoon effect).
9. As soon as a child learns predictability through daily schedules, make a few changes in the schedule so he experiences new things.
10. Make compromises. Allow certain things under certain conditions. Does he always want to talk about the same thing? It will only be allowed in the last 15 minutes of school. Does he want to break glasses? Only in the green container. Jump? On the trampoline, not on the bed. Climb? only up the climbing frame, not up the curtains. Drop objects? Teach him to use a yo-yo or play quoits. In this way, stereotyped activities can be replaced by more harmless activities that serve more or less the same function.
11. Distract him with other activities. Stop the activity (using visual aids) and help the child to start another activity.

I found a good example during a practical training course in Sweden. Lars, a 'terribly' verbal boy with autism (all day long he swore and used obscene language he had learned from others) was not in the habit of doing any school work and he escaped to the toilets any time he felt like it. One day he went and locked himself in there. All the other students begged and pleaded with him to come out, but nothing worked until one of them got the idea of pushing his daily timetable under the door. (Look at the timetable: time to work.) The door opened immediately.

12. Some stereotyped interests can be used constructively, later even built up into a profession. Drawing? Some people with autism earn a good living in this way. Music? One or two can become piano tuners. Interested in food? Maybe there is something he can do in the kitchen. Does he have an interest in water or vacuum cleaners? He may be able to get a job as a cleaner. I know one boy with autism who kept breaking glasses and windows. Now he is a glass blower.

Kanner (1992) wrote about Donald (one of 11 autistic children he described in his study made in 1943) who lived with a farming family:

> When I visited there in May 1945, I was amazed at the wisdom of the couple who took care of him. They managed to give him goals for his stereotypes. They made him use his preoccupation with measurements by having him dig a well and report on its depth. When he kept collecting dead birds and bugs, they gave him a spot for a 'graveyard' and had him put up markers; on each he wrote a first name, the type of animal as a middle-name, and the farmer's last name e.g.: 'John Snail Lewis. Born, date unknown. Died, (date on which he found the animal). When he kept count-ing rows of corn over and over, they had him count the rows while plowing them. On my visit, he plowed six long rows, it was remarkable how well he handled the horse and plow and turned the horse around. It was obvious that they were gently firm.

However, a specialized and carefully individualized full-time autism programme is, and remains, more important than all these individual tips.

2.4. 'Treating' autism: preparation for a meaningful life

There are no therapies needed, there are no tricks to prepare some-one with autism to lead a life as meaningful as possible. Holding therapy, music therapy, underwater therapy, dolphin therapy, tram-poline therapy, wet-sheet therapy, the most crazy things you can imagine exist in the world of autism. There are no limits to the way in which despair can be taken advantage of. None of this has anything to do with understanding autism and, through this, treating it:

There was no sudden 'awakening', no clap of thunder that changed our son into a 'normal' person. It was hard work and it took time. Everything had to be named, its function described. Many things still to do.

Mrs Barron, 1992

To do that you need sufficient means and that is a political question. Society must be prepared to help the most vulnerable people by putting the necessary means at their disposal. Meanwhile all we can do is to help our people with autism on their way to the best of our ability.

Let us be quite clear about this: most of the behavioural problems of people with autism are an expression of suffering, of failure. Those with behaviour problems are not happy with themselves. The best way of treating behaviour problems is to prevent them. You must try to enter the mind of someone with autism, you must try to imagine what is difficult and confusing for him and try to avoid these problems. Professionals who understand what autism entails can then start to organize classes or living groups. (It is with due respect that I have chosen not to mention parents – they are the experts on their own children and must be listened to with total seriousness, but you can not burden them with the entire weight of specialized autism treatment and education.) Along with this, the environment should be specially adapted for autism. Within this special environment you can develop individualized activities; the more success there is, the less stereotyped the behaviour. For the development of individualized activities you need a good assessment as a starting point. Why?

In the short term you must have a clear insight into the skills of the pupil with autism: which skills he has grasped (which ones are successful), which are too difficult (failures) and which ones he is coming to terms with (emerging skills). The 'passes' can best be used for the development of independent work – critical in the preparation of a meaningful adulthood.

The 'emerging skills' could be taught on a one-to-one basis. If you set up activities without a thorough evaluation first, you risk working constantly at the 'failure' level and will, without realizing it, be setting up activities over the child's head, making it very difficult for the pupil with autism. And with no suitable work behaviour, more behavioural problems will occur. If people constantly gave you work that was too difficult for you and for which you were not properly prepared, you would have such problems too. Such evaluations also help us to learn about the pupil's interests. The more activities we can give him based on his own interests, the greater the chance of

motivating him to work. This too is true for all of us. Clear insight
into skills levels, then, is an important element in creating a learning
and living environment with a positive climate.

Assessment is also necessary for building cooperation with
parents. You involve them in assessment at the level they choose.
And of course you use the information they give you: how does our
guest with autism communicate at home? Do the parents use means
of communication other than words to make things clear to him?
How do they say 'no'? It is also important to know the parents' priorities. Assessment will, of course, lead to the development of an individualized educational programme, but which skills do they want
most to see developed? The educational responsibility will finally
come to rest with them; their child is with us only temporarily.

Finally, assessment is needed for the development of skills necessary in adulthood. Which skills does someone with autism need to
feel fulfilled himself when he is an adult (that is, being as happy as
possible in an adapted working and living environment)? Communication, social skills, free-time skills, work skills and work behaviour
skills, self-help and domestic skills and, for the high-functioning pupil
with autism, academic functional skills. Here, again, a thorough
evaluation is essential because of the uneven learning profile of
people with autism and because we see that they can develop different skills in different environments. We return to that theme because
it is so important for good autism treatment and education.

In the chapter on cognition in particular, we pointed out that
people with autism think much less flexibly than we do, that they
often make very concrete links between peoples and places, instead
of giving a new flexible answer appropriate to the situation. Here we
have a boy who only works well in the classroom if his teacher is
wearing a grey sweater. Here we have a boy who loves his daddy
when he is wearing his glasses. Here we have a girl who sings 'Here
comes the Bride' whenever she sees a large chestnut tree (she was
once at a wedding where the couple stood under a chestnut tree
when that song was sung). We all know pupils who use communication cards at school but not in the home, who can ask for fruit juice at
home but not at school, who do exercises at school but not at home,
and so on.

Sometimes these observations lead to the old clichés: 'You see, he
can do it but he isn't motivated enough.' Or sometimes they lead to
an unfortunate atmosphere of rivalry between the professionals and
the parents, particularly at the start of their work together. The
parents feel guilty (he can do more at school than at home) or the

teachers feel inferior to the parents (he will do it at home but not at school). In fact all these paradoxes are part of autism.

We have talked about the difficulties in 'seeing beyond the perception', of overcoming the 'literal'. The perception fixation often limits people with autism in their attempts to make 'spontaneous' generalizations. They associate one skill with a single person, a single room, a small perceptual detail. Their basis of understanding is too narrow to make more spontaneous generalizations possible.

Someone with autism, for example, will learn to communicate in the speech therapy room twice a week and then associate communication with the speech therapist in that particular room. He does not understand that the new words/cards can also be used in other circumstances with other people. Communication is not generalized enough. Since we have come to understand this problem of people with autism better, we have asked our 'specialists' (speech therapists, ergotherapists, physiotherapists) to try to integrate their specialities more into daily life. We ask them to teach the child to communicate not only in the speech therapy room, but also in other situations where they will need to communicate as well. Now our speech therapists are more and more involved in the work sessions, free-time periods, during meals, and so on. These are, after all natural environments for using communication. The 'specialists' remain specialists but integrate their knowledge into the entire structure of daily life. Their attitude becomes that of a 'generalist'.

This incomplete generalization of skills is not limited only to communication but can be found throughout the entire range of skills (free time, social skills, work skills, spending time alone). This has serious consequence, for adult life, unless it is tackled directly. Looked at in this way the 'limited repertory' of adult skills is not simply the result of the limitations due to the combination of mental retardation and autism, but is perhaps also the result of professional neglect. Did we make enough of an effort of teach them the necessary skills when faced with different people and different environments? If they don't make spontaneous generalizations, we should prepare generalization programmes for them. Once they have learned a new skill at school or in the living group, the education process is not over, it is just beginning.

Generalizing at a 'horizontal' level means 'are they able to use their skills in a variety of environments and people?' For example, if someone can ask his teacher for a glass of orange juice at school, can he also do it at home, asking his parents, brothers and sisters? Can he do it at the children's home too? The generalization of key skills is, in fact, even more important than developing new skills.

Such an active orientation towards generalization demands excellent coordination between the various environments, and in practice this is not so simple. Just to name one obstacle, the school and the children's home often have different administrations. It is not a given fact that the two administrations have the same training and motivation to meet the special needs of people with autism appropriately. It is also asking a lot of teachers (who often work in difficult situations with an autism class) to find the time and energy to set up far-reaching cooperation with parents.

And yet cooperation with parents is not simply a question of courtesy. Those who do not try to work with parents in generalizing skills have not really understood this aspect of autism: the special cognitive style of people with autism increases the risk that skills are not used spontaneously in other situations, or with people other than those in the original learning environment. You might say that people with autism have a tendency to 'freeze', to stagnate in a 'limited behaviour repertoire'.

A proper understanding of this serious cognitive limitation now brings us to another challenge: the generalization of skills 'vertically' – coordinating the educational efforts made during school and, later, in adult life. In Chapter 1 I pointed out that the creation of specialized continuity for people with autism is one of the most important consequences of understanding autism as a 'pervasive development disorder'. Meanwhile we have come to understand that people with autism learn functional skills slowly, more slowly than those with a similar developmental level. This is due to their extra difficulty with communication and social perception, and – as we see here again – with the serious difficulties they have with spontaneous generalization. A thorough understanding of this serious 'learning disorder' points inevitably to the necessity of a long-term cooperation between the 'school environment' and the 'work and living environment' in adulthood.

Keeping these points in mind I would like to return to the subject of specialized training and education for autistic people. This begins with the work corner, then attempts to generalize this experience and extend it into other environments to prepare the individual for as meaningful a future as possible.

The work corner is the first place a person with autism begins to feel competent. He is given individual attention with which he will 'learn to learn' and later 'learn to work'. Finally, he will learn to work independently in his work corner, an environment created to be as simple and clear as possible. Here, too, he learns to use visual aids as a support, first trying them in the work corner for work skills (the tasks most easily visualized). We will also give him 'simplified and clarified' tasks that are important for the development of his ability to cope, free-time skills, communication, social skills, etc.

After that we will generalize in another environment (although not too drastically at first): we will remain in the classroom but we will move beyond just the work corner. He will now learn to use free-time schedules in the free-time area. By now he knows his environment so well that he does not need to fall back on his stereotyped behaviour so often. His behaviour shows us that he still needs directed activities even in his 'free-time'. He will now use visual aids for household activities: washing-up, setting the table, clearing away, hanging up the washing, packing his bag . . . He is still in the autism class, but a little less protected. When he is ready the application area will be extended further: beyond the autism class but within the protected environment of the school where there is an autism expert present. The student will see that the table in the canteen is different from the one in the classroom, but that you can set it by following the same principles. He will also learn to react to the instructions of other teachers and do activities with other children. Finally, the moment arrives when he can wash up, clear away, go to 'work' outside school. The number of 'apprenticeships' that he does outside will gradually increase. The magic years between 18 and 21, when he will have to become as independent as possible, are quickly approaching. There is no time to lose.

Things work in phases. In the first phase the child's training and education are, above all, 'developmentally oriented'. This means that parents and professionals are primarily trying to understand the autistic child, to know what he can and cannot do and that he is able to do a little compared with ordinary children. Through this they begin to realize that someone with autism is unusual but not completely alien. The groundwork will now determine the first stage of a realistic educational programme, through which the 'pupil' will learn such things as paying attention, concentrating on the main issues, working independently, communicating and playing; all the things that ordinary children learn spontaneously must be taught explicitly. He must learn to learn. At the same time his strong points and interests should be used to advantage. It is also important that parents and professionals develop some insight into his 'learning style': how does he learn most easily?

It is soon apparent that even verbal children do not respond well
to a merely verbal teaching method. They may understand a
number of instructions, but to work independently, they still need the
strong support of visual aids. It helps greatly to teach by physically
helping the child with new tasks, doing the exercises together to
begin with. For example, the teacher can stand behind him and
physically move him, placing her hands on his arm or hand – four
hands to do the exercise (if the teacher is facing him the information
is less clear: who should do the exercise, him or the teacher? Her
hands and arms make a mirror image of the movement. And what
should he do with the information coming from her mouth and eyes?
Is this also part of the exercise?) For certain children with autism with
a low level of development, the physical method of teaching is sometimes the only one that will work at first.

In the second phase early training and education become much
more functional. Progress is compared less with 'ordinary' development and more with the autism criteria themselves, and it is looked
at in terms of adult needs, work skills, living skills and free-time skills.
The selection of skills to be taught becomes more important and
more urgent. It is now clear that choices must be made: alas, it is
impossible to teach everything. The decisions are best made by a
team of specialists: the parents, those teachers who have monitored
the child's progress over the years, the current teachers and certainly
those responsible for the sheltered living and working facilities for
adults in the district.

Non schola, sed vita discimus: we learn for life, not for school. This is
just as apt for pupils with autism, but what sort of adult life are we
preparing them for? Which level of protection will most likely be
needed? That must be discussed with all those concerned and a
phased plan must be drawn up. The skills learned by the pupil will
then be applied more and more in other environments, at first at
school, then outside the classroom and eventually in the living and
workplaces themselves.

The classroom now starts to look increasingly like a workplace.
Tasks similar to those found in a workplace are set up and similar
routines are installed. There are also more distractions: the radio is
playing in the classroom just as it does in a real workplace. The pupil
has first learned to work in a sheltered environment but now that
environment is being 'normalized'. He is watched carefully to see
whether he can cope with this more casual environment. Skill levels
– successful, failed, developing – remain just as important as they
were before, and the programmes are just as individualized. Interests

are also just as important as they were. But now the question arises as to whether they can be turned into a real job skill for full- or part-time work in the future.

In the third phase there is the realization that the teaching will soon come to an end. The umbilical cord that attaches the pupil to the educational world will soon be cut. The entire educational process must now be fully geared up to future living and work possibilities.

'The right to suitable work' is just as important to the adult as 'the right to a suitable education' is for the child. The major obstacle is that a specialization in autism for the care of adults is much rarer than that for children. Let us be very clear: people with autism will not be able to cope in the adult world without special provisions, without an environment suited to their needs, without proper assessment, without a visual manifestation of a time schedule or visual back-up for their activities.

Jessie seems most normal and is happiest when she is involved with work.

Clara Park, 1986

If things were as they should be, and as they will be in a society adapted to autism, the pupil with autism will, during this third phase, spend much more time in his future work and living place. He will be assessed continuously to ensure that he is able to do the required tasks, that he can follow the routine and show correct work behaviour.

Now the purpose of all the work done in the classroom becomes clear. Thanks to his good 'learning habits', he now also has good 'work habits': he can work independently, cope with changes, follow daily timetables. If there are difficulties he can always be taken aside by the teachers. Desirable behaviour, skills and routines are again taught within a sheltered environment and then generalizations are retaught. Obviously, there must be a desire to make the necessary adaptations to that future environment. In it people should be aware that 'different' people need a 'different' environment. They understand that it is mainly a question of courtesy: the stronger make greater concessions towards the weaker. It works, down to the last detail, and it is to everyone's advantage.

In my opinion the efforts of professionals and parents should be spent primarily on looking for a suitable working environment. The happiness of an adult with autism depends more on the sort of individualized occupation he has during the day than on where he sleeps at night. Living and working facilities should be separate so that the adult 'goes to work' like everyone else. This plea for their work, is however, based on ethical considerations different from our own. The adult with autism needs to feel his own worth, he needs to be independently occupied with activities he can cope with and not always be dependent on people and events beyond his control. This means that there should be more successes and fewer failures. The adult need not always fall back on his stereotyped behaviour as now he has something to replace it with, and what is more, something that is more meaningful.

This sketch of continuity in specialized autism facilities might seem like science fiction. But the knowledge is there. It only remains to be put it into practice. All that we have written about the link between understanding and education in autism, moreover, is so logical that common sense will surely win eventually. It is just a matter of time.

But what about the people with autism who are now adult, who have lost out on time? Experience shows that it is not too late even for them. It can never be too late to be surrounded for the first time by people who really understand their handicap, in an adapted environment, with individualized programmes through which they can learn to communicate. The age of adults corresponds to the third phase, but because of opportunities missed in the past they often have to 'earn and learn' (like children in the first phase). This may seem discouraging, but there is hope for the future. A great deal of pent-up hopelessness and despair can be channelled into other streams. It is never too late.

Special facilities without a proper specialization in autism can often be more of a hindrance than a help. The continuity sketched here, in three phases, does not lead to a cure but to dignity and to a realistic balance between integration and segregation. The choice is not based on abstract moral principles but is determined by the abilities of the individual with autism himself, helped by our special provisions for his needs. The choice must be individualized in every case. Never integration at any price – a price which is paid by the handicapped person himself –but 'optimal' integration in which a realistic balance is found between our world and their world, between his adaptation via an individualized educational programme and ours, via the constant adaptation of the environment, assessment, activities.

But let us never forget that the most important adaptations must come from us.

Appendix: Ian

A happy family

When our Ian was born he was our sixth child. We had three boys and three girls; the oldest son was seventeen, the oldest daughter was sixteen. Everyone adored Ian, he was definitely not an unwanted child as the doctors later both thought and said. We lived in an old farmhouse with a big garden and we had five bedrooms. There was plenty of room for another child. That summer we were a happy family.

Ian helped us get over our depression

On December third, when Ian was almost ten months old, our eldest son was killed in an accident on the way to school. The world stood still for us. We looked in amazement at other people who could still talk and laugh. Our old world was in ruins and poor Ian, he saw nothing but sad faces and dark colours day in day out, even though he had always loved clothes with flowers on them – he used to look at them and feel them . . . Later when we found out that there was something abnormal about Ian, I had the suspicion that it had something to do with the nasty experience of the death of his brother. It took us years to get over it; in a way Ian helped us to get over it – the more difficult he became, the more the death of our eldest faded into the background.

'Come on, Ian, we're going to eat some nice cake . . .'

Our other children were early talkers. Ian wasn't, though . . . When he was eighteen months old, he was ill. I made up a bed for him on the sofa and wanted to tuck him in. Ian wriggled out. I tried to tuck him in several times until he got angry and screamed, 'Sit!' He wanted to sit up and if it was really necessary he could say so.

When he was around eight years old, he was always running away. We had to look for him for hours, sometimes until the middle of the night. That was why we always locked the front door and the gate. One afternoon I was doing the ironing, I had slippers on with very thin soles. Then our son Robert let one of his friends out. A little later I started to wonder if he had locked the door. I went to have a look and saw the front door open and Ian, further down the street, standing and watching. I called 'Come on, Ian, we're going to have some nice cake', but he didn't listen. With the front door still open, and the iron still on, we then started a marathon which lasted for hours. Every time I started to run, I lost my slippers and he managed to get away. At every crossroad he knew which way to go to get further from home. When we came to yet another crossroad with about 15 metres between us Ian turned round and shouted, 'Mummy over there', and pointed in the direction of the house. He wanted me to go back home, and if I hadn't been so tired and miserable I would have been happy because Ian had just said 'Mummy' for the first time in his life.

Meanwhile Robert was reading in his room and my husband was working in the fields. I started to wonder if I had left the iron standing up. It was only hours later that I was lucky enough to see my nephew's father-in-law. He realised what was going on, chased Ian on his bicycle and caught him. Then he stopped a car and asked the driver to take us home. He agreed and I'm still grateful to him. By then it was ten in the evening, my husband had come home from the fields, had his dinner and was weeding the vegetable garden. The iron was still on – it hadn't occurred to anyone to turn it off. I was so angry with Robert and my husband because neither of them had even thought of getting into the car and coming to look for us, that once I had put Ian into bed I crawled into bed myself. We were both so tired that we didn't want anything to eat, and for all I cared the iron could stay on all night.

On clouds and eating problems

One evening around half past ten we couldn't find Ian. We looked all over the house, in all the barns and the outhouses. He was nowhere to be found. It was winter, cold and dark, and he didn't have many clothes on. We started to panic. Then I went to look in the garden.

Ian was standing there, right at the bottom of the path with his head back looking at the full moon.

He was always very attracted to lights. He could look straight into the sun. I wanted to stop him. 'No, Ian, you'll hurt your eyes.' When a cloud moved in front of the sun he would get very angry. He would grab my hand and throw it in the air. I was supposed to take away the veil that was covering the sun. For years he thought of my hands as an extension of his. At one time this was so bad that it was almost impossible to do the housework, never mind help on the farm. He dragged me round everywhere to do everything for him. I couldn't escape.

It got better when he found a heap of sand against a wall. It had just rained and the sand was wet. He threw some against the wall and it stuck until it started to dry and slowly fall off. All that summer he sat in that sand. I was to see that it stayed wet because dry sand doesn't stick and then he would scream bloody murder. During that period he would eat hardly any soup, vegetables or anything. We couldn't get it into him. The children's doctor said he had to eat twice a day because he was so weak from just drinking milk. I mixed up soup, vegetables, meat and potatoes into a thick porridge and then we needed two people to hold him. Every time he opened his mouth to scream I got a spoonful into him. It was a sad affair but it was the only way. Until he discovered the sand. Then it was easy. While Ian was busy throwing the sand, I went outside with my bowl and spooned it into his mouth. In ten minutes he had eaten the lot without a fuss. But I don't think he knew he had eaten. A few weeks later things had changed so much that as soon as he heard the mixer (it was summer and the door stayed open), he rushed inside. Then he would pull and tug me because he wanted to eat at once. It went so far that I hardly dared use the mixer for the soup because he screamed bloody murder if there wasn't anything for him to eat.

Nothing abnormal about his eyes

When Ian was one, we went to a children's doctor. He didn't see anything abnormal until Ian was about three and a half. Then he sent us to an eye specialist because he thought there was something wrong with Ian's eyes – he always looked through people. The specialist declared that small children were never afraid of him because he never wore a white coat which frightened them. This was true until he stretched out his hands to Ian who started to fight for his life. Eventually he had to call on his wife so we could both hold him and he could look into Ian's eyes. The result: nothing abnormal about his eyes.

Ian couldn't stand anything being moved in the house. Cleaning was a nightmare. If I moved the table and chairs to one side to scrub the other side, he began to scream and pull everything back to its place in the middle of my soapy wet floor. For a few years I would get up at four in the morning while everyone was still asleep, just to try to clean without making any noise because if he woke up he came straight downstairs and the whole thing started again.

Well, I never! What's going on here?

My grandmother often used to drop in. She thought that I had spoiled Ian rotten and that she could teach him to listen. She walked behind shouting at him loudly and Ian laughed for joy. He thought Granny was playing with him. After an hour of this, Granny was out of breath and shouted crossly, 'Now I'm going home, naughty boy.'

One summer Ian spent all his time rolling the blinds up and down and playing with the light switch. Off and on, off and on. My grandmother came in and said, 'Well, I never! What's going on here? We can't have this!' and Granny started to pull up all the blinds. While she was pulling up the second one, Ian let down the first one. He was dancing and chuckling with laughter and Granny pulled and pulled. After a quarter of an hour she had had enough and went home, angry again.

Sandwiches yes, sandwiches no

When Ian was four we took him to the nursery school in the village just for the afternoon. Up till then Ian had never eaten a sandwich. He refused to eat bread so I didn't give him any sandwiches to take with him. After a few days the teacher asked me to give Ian a sandwich for playtime because he took the other children's sandwiches from them and ate them. That was good, it was something new he had learned there and afterwards he also wanted to eat bread at home.

Ian liked going to the nursery school but after a while they asked me to keep an eye on him at home because when the other children built towers with the building blocks, Ian rushed round the classroom knocking them down having fun while the other children started to cry.

'Mary, Ian is riding his bicycle with nothing on'

One afternoon about half past twelve, I was getting him ready to go
to school, washing him and putting clean clothes on him, when I saw
that I didn't have any clean underpants downstairs, I went upstairs to
get some but when I came down the kitchen door was locked. I could
only go outside. That day my husband and his brother were sowing.
I had hoped that they would be home before one so that my husband
could take Ian to school. But now I was standing at the kitchen
window asking Ian nicely, 'Please open the door so mummy can
come in.'

At first Ian jumped around laughing but after that he really tried
to turn the key in the lock. I could see through the window that he
couldn't manage it. He wasn't quite so happy then. At that point my
grandmother arrived. I explained what had happened and she
started to shout through the kitchen window. 'Ian, open that door at
once or I'll give you a good hiding!' Ian fled into the living room and
hid.

Then the sowers came home. My brother-in-law broke out some
stones around the cellar window and climbed down into the cellar.
Luckily the cellar door was not locked. Ian was so happy when we
could get in again. That night it was almost impossible to get him to
bed.

He usually slept a bit in the mornings. One morning when I
thought he was still asleep, my youngest sister (Aunt Nina) and her
daughter turned up on their bicycles. Our Ian was with them on his
bicycle and he was wearing Marleen's shoes, trousers and a blouse.
They were laughing and laughing. That morning Ian had woke up
early, taken off his pyjamas and ridden naked to Aunt Nina's (nearly
a mile away). Marleen had seen him coming and had called, 'Mum,
come and look who's coming!'

That summer Ian liked to walk around with nothing on. I had
real problems stopping him from taking his clothes off. One time the
neighbour's children ran around shouting loudly, 'Mary, Ian has
ridden off on his bicycle and he has nothing on!' Ian was only about
six years old so it wasn't so bad, but I collected some trousers and a
sweater and rode after him.

The same summer by chance Ian discovered that you could get
sweets from the corner shop. He walked in, took what he wanted and
walked out again. The shopkeeper tried to take them all away from
him but it was hopeless. I made an agreement with her. She wrote
down what Ian took and I paid her for it next time I went into the

shop. This time Ian had ridden to the shop and was on his way home. He had both feet on the ground and was taking wrappers off all the sweets. All the people in the street were staring at him as if it were the end of the world.

'If he were mine, he would get a good hiding'

Around this time we stopped going out. We stayed away from church, we stayed at home when there was something happening like the village feast, the harvest supper, etc. and we hardly ever went to visit the family. Everywhere it was the same thing: 'If he were one of mine he would be spanked.'

Our vicar said that it didn't disturb him and that we were still welcome at church. But when you knew that you were the centre of the whole church's attention, when everyone looked at Ian and you sat there sweating with irritation, and when you knew that if you said anything it would make things even worse, you didn't really feel like going. Ian went to see my two sisters sometimes. He knew where he was welcome. And if he saw my sister's husband, he was really happy. He would say 'Hello Uncle Jeff, hello Uncle Jeff.' He was really pleased to see Uncle Jeff.

We often bought toys for Ian but usually he didn't do anything with them. Our eldest daughter once bought him a duck on wheels. He must have been about three years old. He kept pushing the duck down the cellar stairs, over and over. I told him that the duck would break on the stone steps but he didn't listen. Then I heard him crying downstairs in the cellar. He was sitting crying on the bottom step with the broken duck in his arms. Now I realise that I always talked too much to Ian and he didn't understand. Now we realise that a person with autism finds it difficult to understand language but what did we know then?

When Ian was about four years old he made a bus with blocks on the sofa. He then wanted to build from there down to the floor but of course the blocks just fell. He cried and cried. I tried to help him by building a tower from the bottom to the top but he didn't want that. It had to go from above downwards and that was that. After crying for an hour (I went on with my housework), he came round. He made a bus with toys in the kitchen and later, another bus with my pots and pans and my husband's tools – that went faster because the pieces were bigger. He was so happy! He looked at his work with a big smile of satisfaction. I told everyone to leave everything alone, that it all should stay where it was until the next day. Then he could play to his heart's content all afternoon and evening. He slept late next morning and when he woke up he didn't mind that everything had been tidied up.

When he was six, Ian went to a boarding school at X. When he came home one Friday night, he put a ladder against one of the out buildings and started to try and pull off the guttering. Of course he wasn't allowed to do that, much to Ian's great sorrow. The next Monday we knew why he had done this: at X they had renewed the guttering the week before.

'But your son is looking for you, Ma'am'

It wasn't so busy on the farm in August and then I would take Ian to the beach for two or three days. He enjoyed that very much. We took a coach and usually some of the family came with us – my mother or my sister or a niece. We did that for years, but once when he was seventeen just the two of us went, Ian and me. My husband never wanted to come.

We rented two deckchairs. Ian hardly ever stayed in his chair, he went for a paddle or played in the sand. At five o'clock we went to get something to eat. When we came back to our chairs they were no longer in the sun and it was chilly. I said, 'Ian, I'm just going to put the chairs in the sun because it's too cold here.' Then I started to move my bags and the chairs. I looked around and Ian was nowhere to be seen. That is when the misery started. He had probably seen from a distance that I was not where we had been and had gone to look for me. I went to look for him. We must have been going round in circles and missed each other. A lot of people I stopped and asked, said, 'But your son is looking for you, he was here a minute ago.'

At about seven o'clock the beach started to empty but Ian was nowhere to be found. I went back to the parking place and told the bus driver, 'I've lost Ian.' He gave me a funny look but didn't say anything. I was terribly afraid that Ian had fallen into the hands of a gang of lads who were teasing him. Then I went back and traced all our steps – where we had been to eat at lunch time and at tea time, on the beach, everywhere. After that I asked where the police station was and walked there. I felt like the most unhappy mother in all the world.

I sat in that police station for hours. I didn't dare to ring home – my husband panics so quickly and he couldn't do anything to help me anyway. All of a sudden a policeman came in and said they had found Ian, he was on the Redcar Road, they were bringing him back to Scarborough. Ian had gone to the parking place, seen that the bus had left, thought that I was on it and had started to walk home. I am sure that if everyone had left him alone he would have got home. I don't know how many days it would have taken though . . . When the policeman came back with Ian he couldn't stop laughing with joy and I was so glad to see him. Then I phoned my husband to tell him that Ian had been lost but was now found and we'd get the next train home. Unfortunately there aren't many trains at night. We stood in a couple of stations for ages. We were cold because we weren't dressed to be out at night. Anyway, we arrived home at half past two in the morning. That was the last time we went on a trip with that coach company.

What happens to Ian now?

Ian is now an adult and is in a home at Z. It has more structure than other homes but otherwise it is the same as the others. The carers come and go and, in spite of good intentions, they make many mistakes.

Ian spends most of his time walking around nervously and has fits of rage. When he first went there was one carer who understood him and Ian felt happy with him. But he was actually an occupational therapist and he left when he found a job in his own field. Ian felt as if his world had collapsed and they couldn't do anything with him. He was given nine pills a day, though later they reduced the dosage. Now he is given only one pill in the evenings as far as I know. The doctor says that this medicine is not dangerous, but I think that all doctors say all medicines are good until it is proven that there are major side effects.

A few years ago, Ian went camping. Dorothy, the social worker who went with him, explained everything using photos and drawings. Ian enjoyed it so much. They couldn't stop talking about the way he had changed there, how enthusiastically he joined in. But when the week was over Ian fell into a black mood, you could see disappointment written on his face.

A few weeks ago they also started to use photos and drawings in Z. They made a board with drawings for everything he had to do in the morning: wash, shave, make the bed. Ian was pleased and the carers were pleased. Suddenly there were no problems with shaving – before that he often used to come home unshaven. Then all of a sudden something was wrong. Ian tore the drawings off the board. They made him draw them again himself which helped. At the time they were cleaning the house and collecting dead wood and burning it. Ian went inside and took his board and threw it on the bonfire. What had happened? Why did he want to get rid of the drawings and the board all of a sudden? Knowing Ian, my guess is that one of the carers approached it the wrong way one morning and then he didn't want to use it any more.

Last winter on a Sunday when Ian was at home, John, the thirteen-year-old son of my sister Lydia came in with a synthesiser, a musical instrument that you can play yourself, with all sorts of knobs which make music. John began to play it. Then Ian came in and started to play it himself with such a happy expression. I'd never seen him so enthusiastic. I knew at once what to buy Ian for his birthday. Now he would have something to make him happy in his room at Z. He would have something to do instead of just lying on his bed. A few days later I rang Z to ask them if Ian was happy with his music. The carers were very enthusiastic about the possibilities of such a small instrument. Because it was such an expensive instrument they had to put it away they said, so that Ian could play it only once a week. The result? Ian refuses to touch it any more. Ian is disappointed, the carers are disappointed and we are disappointed.

At the parent's weekend at the Autism Society, a social worker was trying a sort of sliding puzzle, one of those things with squares you have to push into the right place. Ian stood next to her, nervously biting on his thumb. All of a sudden he took it from her and in a couple of seconds he had everything in the right place. We have often found that he has an insight into technical things which would be the envy of many normal people.

What will happen to Ian? He will have to take tranquillizers all his life. We are now 64 and 69 years old and who knows how long our health will hold up, how long we will live. We can only hope that there will always be carers who know about autism, who want to learn more, who don't immediately think that they know best and yet, despite good intentions, continue to make a mess of things. We also hope that our other children will not abandon Ian when we are no longer here.

I forgot something. A few months ago we bought a new TV. It has about 60 channels on it. You can change the channels with a remote control but there are only nine numbers on it and lots of things which to me are incomprehensible. But Ian came home, looked at it and immediately knew how it worked. He likes channel 22 best but I can't get beyond channel 9.

Bibliography

The following references have been selected and are meant to offer a general orientation.

Chapter 1

Akerley, M. (1987). What's in a name? In: E. Schopler, and G. Mesibov (Eds), *Diagnosis and Assessment in Autism*. New York: Plenum Press.

American Psychiatric Association (1994). *Diagnostic and Statistical Manual of Mental Disorders* (DSM IV) Washington DC: American Psychiatric Press.

Gillberg, C. (1990). Autism and pervasive developmental disorders. *Journal of Child Psychology and Psychiatry* **31**: 99–119.

Rutter, M. (1983). Cognitive deficits in the pathogenesis of autism. *Journal of Child Psychology and Psychiatry* 24.

Steffenburg, S. (1990). *Neurobiological Correlates of Autism*. N. Göteborg, University of Göteburg.

World Health Organisation (1987). *International Classification of Diseases* (ICD-10) Ch. 5. Geneva: WHO.

Chapter 2

Attwood, A.H., Fritt, U. and Hermelin, B. (1988). The understanding and use of inter-personal gestures by autistic and Down's syndrome children.

Baron-Cohen, S., Leslie, A.M., and Frith, U. (1985) Does the autistic have a 'theory of mind?' Cognition, **21**

Bruner, J.H. (1974). *Beyond the Information Given*. London: George Allen and Unwin.

Frith, U. (1989). *Autism: Explaining the Enigma*. Oxford: Basil Blackwell,.

Hermelin, B. (1978). Images and language. In: M. Rutter and E. Schopler (Eds), *Autism, A Reappraisal of Concepts and Treatment*. New York: Plenum Press.

Hermelin, B. and O'Connor, N. (1970). *Psychological Experiments with Autistic Children*. Oxford: Pergamon Press.

Mesibov, G., Troxler, M. and Boswell, S. (1988). Assessment in the classroom. In: E. Schopler and G. Mesibov (Eds), 1, *Diagnosis and Assessment in Autism*. New York: Plenum Press.

Peeters, T. (1984). *Uit zichzelf gekeerd*. Nijmegen: Dekker en van de Vegt.

Schopler, E. and Reichler, J.R. (1990). *Individualized Assessment and Treatment for Autistic and*

179

Developmentally Disabled Children, Vol. 2: *Teaching Strategies for Parents and Professionals.* Austin, TX: Pro-Ed (1992).

Schopler, E. *et al.* (1990). *Individualized Assessment and Treatment for Autistic and Developmentally Disabled Children*, Vol. 1: *Psychoeductional Profile–Revised (PEP-R)* . Austin, TX: Pro-Ed.

Shea, V. (1984). Explaining mental retardation and autism to parents. In: E. Schopler and G. Mesibov (Eds), *The Effects of Autism on the Family.* New York: Plenum Press.

Van Berckelaer-Onnes, I. (1992). *Leven naar de letter.* Groningen: Wolters-Noordhoff.

Wing, L. (1984). *Early Diagnosis and the Impact of Autistic Handicap on the Family.* Paris: Autism-Europe.

Chapter 3

Fay, W.H. and Schuler, A. (1980). *Emerging Language in Autistic Children.* London: Edward Arnold.

Grandin, T. and Scariano, M. (1986). *Emergence: Labelled Autistic.* Novato, CA: Arena.

Ionesco, E. (1978). *Story Number 2.* U.S.A: Harlin Quist.

Menyuk, P. and Quill, K. (1985). Semantic problems in autistic children. In: E. Schopler and G. Mesibov (Eds), *Communication Problems in Autism.* New York: Plenum Press.

Prizant, B. and Schuler, A. (1987). Facilitating communication: language approaches. In: D. Cohen and A. Donnellan (Eds), *Handbook of Autism and Pervasive Developmental Disorders.* New York: John Wiley and Sons.

Schopler, E. and Mesibov, G. (Eds), (1985). *Communication Problems in Autism.* New York: Plenum Press.

Schopler, E. and Mesibov, G. (Eds), (1988). *Diagnosis and Assessment in Autism.* New York: Plenum Press.

Schuler, A. and Prizant, B. (1985, 1986). Echolalia. In: E. Schopler and G. Mesibov (Eds), *Communication Problems in Autism.* New York: Plenum Press; Novato, CA: Arena.

Watson, L., Lord, C. *et al.* (1989). *Teaching Spontaneous Communication to Autistic and Developmentally Handicapped Children.* New York: Irvington.

Chapter 4

Dawson, G. (Ed.) (1989). *Autism: Nature, Diagnosis and Treatment.* London: Guilford Press.

Gillberg, C: (1990). Autism and pervasive developmental disorders. *Journal of Child Psychology and Psychiatry* **31**: 99–119.

Grandin, T. and Scariano, M. (1986). *Emergence: Labelled Autistic.* Novato, CA: Arena.

Olley, G. (1986). The TEACCH curriculum for teaching social behaviour to children with autism. In: E. Schopler and G. Mesibov (Eds.), *Social Behaviour in Autism.* New York: Plenum Press.

Mesibov, G. (1990). Normalization and its relevance today. *Journal of Autism and Developmental Disorders* **20**: 3.

Park, C.C. (1986). Social growth in autism: a parent's perspective. In: E. Schopler and G. Mesibov (Eds), *Social Behaviour in Autism.* New York: Plenum Press.

Prizant, B. and Schuler, A. (1987). Facilitating communication: language approaches. In: D. Cohen and A. Donnellan, *Handbook of Autism and Pervasive Developmental Disorders.* New York: John Wiley and Sons.

Quill, K. (1990). A model for integrating children with autism. *Focus on Autistic Behaviour,* **5** (4): 1–19.

Ricks, D. and Wing, L. (1976). Language, communication and the use of symbols. In: L. Wing (Ed.), *Early Childhood Autism*. Oxford: Pergamon Press.

Rutter, M. (1983). Cognitive deficits in the pathogenesis of autism. *Journal of Child Psychology and Psychiatry*: 24

Schopler, E. and Mesibov, G. (Eds), (1986). *Social Behaviour in Autism*. New York: Plenum Press.

Simpson, R. (1993). Successful integration of children and youth with autism in main-streamed settings. *Focus on Autistic Behaviour*. **7**: 1–13.

Steffenburg, S. (1990). *Neurobiological Correlates of Autism*. Goteborg: University of Goteborg.

Van Oosthuysen, E. (1986). Het verhaal van Hans. In: *Autisme en onderwijs*. Gent: Vlaamse Vereniging Autisme.

Volkmar, F. (1986). Compliance, noncompliance and negativism. In: E. Schopler and G. Mesibov (Eds), *Social Behaviour in Autism*. New York: Plenum Press.

Wing, L. (1981). Language, social and cognitive impairments in autism and severe mental retardation. *Journal of Autism and Developmental Disorders* **11**: 31–45.

Wing, L. and Gould, J. (1979). Severe impairments of social interaction and associated abnormalities in children: epidemiology and classification. *Journal of Autism and Developmental Disorders* **9**: 11–29.

Wooten, M. and Mesibov, G. (1986). Social skills training for elementary school autistic children with normal peers. In: E. Schopler and G. Mesibov (Eds), *Social Behaviour in Autism*. New York: Plenum Press.

Chapter 5

Dawson, G. (Ed.) (1989). *Autism: Nature, Diagnosis and Treatment*. London: Guilford Press.

Frith, U. (1989). *Autism, Explaining the Enigma*. Oxford: Basil Blackwell.

Fromberg, R. (1984). The sibling's changing roles. In: E. Schopler and G. Mesibov (Eds), *The Effects of Autism on the Family*. New York: Plenum Press.

Kanner, L. (1992). Follow-up study of eleven autistic children originally reported in 1943. *Focus on Autistic Behaviour* **7** (5): 1–11.

Van Berckelaer-Onnes, I. (1988). Speltraining bij autistische kinderen. *Tijdschrift Kinderjeugdpsychotherapie* **15**: 136–144.

van Bourgondien, M.B. (1993). Behaviour problems in autism. In: E. Schopler, C. Lord and L. Watson (Eds), *Pre-school Issues in Autism*. New York: Plenum Press.

Quotes from people with autism and their parents are drawn from the following sources:

Barron, J. and Barron, S. (1992). *There's a Boy in Here*. New York: Simon and Schuster.

De Clercq, H. 'Dit zijn geen rozen, 't zijn witten. Over een jongen met autisme. Antwerpen: Hadewijch (in preparation).

Grandin, T. (1992). An inside view of autism. In: E. Schopler and G. Mesibov (Eds), *High Functioning Individuals with Autism*. New York: Plenum Press.

Grandin, T. and Scariano, M. (1966). *Emergence Labelled Autistic*. Novato, CA: Arena Press.

Jolliffe, T., Landsdown, R. and Robinson, C. (1992). Autism: a personal account. *Communication* **26** (3),

Sinclair, J. (1992). Bridging the gaps: an inside-out view of autism. In: E. Schopler and G. Mesibov (Eds), *High Functioning Individuals with Autism*. New York: Plenum Press.

Trehin, C. (1993). Les autistes de haut niveau et leurs écrits. ARAPI, **2.**

Index